At Ease

discussing money and values in small groups

John & Sylvia Ronsvalle

with U. Milo Kaufmann

An Alban Institute Publication

The authors gratefully acknowledge permission to reprint from the following:

Biblical Foundations for Small Group Ministry by Gareth Weldon Icenogle. Copyright © 1994 by Gareth Weldon Icenogle. Used by permission of InterVarsity Press, P.O. Box 1400, Downers Grove, IL 60515.

Groups Alive–Churches Alive by Clyde Reid, copyright © 1969 by Clyde Reid. Used by permission of HarperCollins Publishers.

Journey Inward–Journey Outward by Elizabeth O'Connor, copyright © 1968 by Elizabeth O'Connor. Used by permission of HarperCollins Publishers.

Sharing the Journey: Support Groups and America's New Quest For Community by Robert Wuthnow. Copyright © 1994 by Robert Wuthnow. Reprinted with permission of The Free Press, a Division of Simon & Schuster.

Scripture quotations are taken from the following translations:

The Amplified New Testament. Copyright © 1954, 1958, 1987 by The Lockman Foundation. Used by permission.

The King James Version (KJV).

The Holy Bible, New International Version®. NIV®. Copyright © 1973, 1978, 1984 by International Bible Society. Used by permission of Zondervan Publishing House. All rights reserved.

The New Revised Standard Version Bible (NRSV), copyright © 1989 by the Division of Christian Education of the National Council of the Churches of Christ in the U.S.A. Used by Permission. All rights reserved.

The Revised Standard Version (RSV), © 1946, 1952, 1971, Division of Christian Education, National Council of the Churches of Christ in the United States of America.

Library of Congress Catalog Card Number 98-73456
ISBN 1-56699-202-8

CONTENTS

A LITANY

We acknowledge the abundance of our material resources and express our gratitude to God on whom we depend for all good things.

We understand that while we have much, many others in our global community are without the very basics needed to sustain the gift of life.

We confess that our decisions about what we need too often go unexamined, as we give in to the values of the culture around us.

Together recalling Jesus' words, "No one can serve two masters . . . You cannot serve both God and Money," we acknowledge that money has power today to addict, to corrupt, and to destroy those who use it carelessly.

We resolve, with Christ's help, with the guidance of the Holy Spirit, and with the mutual support of each other, to open ourselves to change so that we may work more effectively through our congregation to reach out in love to those who so desperately need our help.

To this end, we commit to explore together—in a candid and caring fashion—our relationship to God and to money.

We rejoice that, with God's help and in Jesus' name, we are able to be part of a movement to end the misery of millions of men, women, and children as we seek to be faithful in our witness in both word and deed.

We affirm the importance of reaching out in love to those in need close to home, even as we grow in our global vision.

God, help us, your children, as we now humble ourselves before you and each other so that—renewed and emboldened—we might better serve in Jesus' name. Amen.

PREFACE

The pastor sounded urgent. He had, he said, shared with the people in his congregation all the information on church giving patterns we had given him. He had discussed both the great need in the world, as well as each person's potential for making a difference. On one level, they seemed to understand how important an issue this was. They had even expressed agreement that church members ought to respond. But somehow they were still not making a meaningful connection between their faith and their own money. He appreciated the materials we had given him so far. Yet, could we possibly provide him with some type of small group structure which would help people integrate their faith and money?

That request began a process for us. Our first step was to talk with knowledgeable folks. Even though one of us has a seminary degree and a master's and Ph.D. in clinical psychology, and the other brings an undergraduate minor in psychology, we still figured Proverbs 15:22 was probably true: "Without counsel, plans go wrong, but with many advisers they succeed" (NRSV).

We are grateful for the early input we received from Thom Moore, a practicing psychologist and active church member. Howard Snyder, a Wesley scholar and seminary professor, also provided both expertise and valuable insights in developing the guide presented in chapter 10.

As we developed the materials, U. Milo Kaufmann, a professor of English literature and church leader with extensive personal, small group experience, played a key role in the small group resource we offer you in this book. He participated in the earliest consultations. He took the first set of 15 questions we wrote and expanded the collection. His unfailing encouragement and shared sense of the desire of church members to make a difference have been vital components of this work.

It was a request from Beth Gaede, acquisitions editor at the Alban Institute, that began the process of turning this congregational resource into a book. Beth asked us to think about a volume for the Institute's series on money. In addition to books that present information and strategies for reaching out to those in need, we've authored books about trends in church giving, through both our numerical analysis reports and through a national study on the underlying factors that affect giving. Now we wondered if more people could benefit from this small group concept that had grown out of a grassroots congregational need.

In addition to the above people, we continue to be grateful to the staff we work with at empty tomb, inc. They share our deep conviction that there is great potential for the church to share God's love with a hurting world. The volunteers and supporters of empty tomb, along with the many concerned individuals we've encountered through our financial discipleship work, convince us that church members want to make a difference in Jesus' name. That gives us the hope to continue to explore all avenues which can help to make that happen.

In particular, we not only acknowledge Milo Kaufmann's many talents and abilities, especially in relationship to his contribution to this volume, but we also thank God for the friendship he and his wife, Helen, have shared with us over the last 28 years.

And you, dear reader, are the reason we offer these ideas. We look forward to sharing a journey of discovery with you, as you use this book to explore your relationship with both God and money!

John and Sylvia Ronsvalle

PART 1

Outline for Adventure

CHAPTER 1

You Are Invited!

Before you read any further, clear your mind. Step back from your busy day. Settle yourself in your chair comfortably. Raise and drop your shoulders and breathe evenly ten times. Are you feeling a little more relaxed?

Now we want you to think about feelings you have about a certain concept. As you read this word, try to identify what emotions best describe your response to it. Ready?

The word is: money. Think carefully. What did you feel?

Write it in this space if you like: _____.

Maybe you didn't have just one emotion. What did you feel? Excitement? A thrill? Lust, maybe? Or envy? Anger? Or did you feel guilt? Perhaps you felt confusion. Or maybe you had a vague sense of great possibilities.

Money is a complicated idea. We love it, and yet sometimes we hate it. We want more and when we get more, it never seems to be enough.

Whatever you felt, you can be sure that nobody else had exactly the same feelings as you did. That's because nobody else has lived your life, had your experiences, and come to this point in time with the same combination of nature and nurture that you have.

Our feelings about money are often hard to explain. Even many married couples find it difficult to make each other understand what they think about the topic. There may be no other part of our lives where we are so alone as we are in our relationship to our money.

We're writing this book to help you with that loneliness, that sense of isolation that we all feel when we think about money.

Your Unique Journey

We're also inviting you on an adventure. Instead of exploring a new land or the bottom of the ocean or infinite space, we're inviting you on another kind of journey. It's a journey of discovery nevertheless. And what you'll find is not already decided, because you are unlike anyone else. When you work through the following pages you will be exploring uncharted territory. You'll be reflecting on why you think about money as you do. You'll try to find out what parts of money are important to you. And you'll develop fresh ways of looking at the role that money plays in your life.

The chapter on "How to Use this Book," suggests that you can use these pages as a personal reflection exercise. You can read through the pages and do the exercises in the privacy of your home if you like.

However, may we suggest that you take a few friends with you on this journey you are about to begin? You can travel these strange roads together. It's always a good idea to explore unfamiliar surroundings with trusted companions. As the writer of Ecclesiastes observed, "Two are better than one . . . For if they fall, one will lift up the other" (Eccles. 4:9-10, NRSV).

Before you actually set out, we want to provide you with preparation for your journey. By reflecting on the series of questions in chapters 5 through 7, you are going to be rethinking a lot of ideas that are so familiar that they seem to be facts rather than assumptions. Most of these discussion topics ask you to reflect on your personal experiences and views on money. However, it might be a good idea to lay a shared foundation for the road we are about to travel together.

So first, let's look at a very basic idea: What is money?

Simple Economics?

We observe two distinguished men sitting in a men's club, as the cartoonist has drawn it. They are apparently in the middle of a conversation. Dressed in business suits, the one with graying temples is lighting a pipe. The other, seated comfortably, looks at his friend and says, "All right, Stan. Let's accept for the sake of argument your preposterous notion that money isn't everything."

Not everything? But it sure is a lot! As singer Pearl Bailey said, "I've been poor and I've been rich, and honey, rich is better."

Money makes people "rich" in a lot of ways. At its most basic, money is a medium of exchange. You spend yourself in an activity. In exchange, you receive pieces of paper and perhaps some coins. You are able to take these papers to a store and trade them in for the product of someone else's activity. The more money you have, the more items you can buy. No questions asked. What a handy system!

Imagine if we did not have such a medium of exchange. In that case, you would have to have a series of what are called "double coincidences." You would have to carry around what you made with your own hands until you ran into someone who had something you wanted. Now, when you found the person who was carrying around what you wanted, this other person would have to want what *you* made in order for a trade to result. A monetary system removes the need for you to find the particular person who has exactly what you want just when you want it. You trade your work in for symbols of credit. Then you can use those symbols anywhere you like.

So money can make people rich in the ability to buy possessions, if having a lot of things is one definition of being "rich." We expend ourselves, accumulate pieces of paper, and then trade in this paper for things we want to have.

If that was all money was, of course, it probably would not be so complicated. But there is more to money than simply economics. Money can make people rich in a way that has far more impact than meeting a specific need for food or clothing.

Money Is . . .

For one thing, in a very real sense, our money is *us*. We have invested ourselves in some activity, mentally and/or physically, and in exchange received these pieces of paper. When we look at money, we are looking at our invested energy made tangible. In that sense, our money is our stored time and talent. Any discussion of money needs to recognize that we are not talking about stacks of bills or numbers on a page. At some deep level, discussing money taps into how we—and our ancestors— have invested our time and energy. There is a close personal identification that is tied up with our own sense of worth and how we are valued by others.

Money also represents *possibilities*. What these possibilities are depends on who you are and what is important to you. For some people, the most important thing they could have is security. They don't want a lot of stuff or to control other people. What they want is to be sure life hands them no surprises, or if it does, that they're ready for them. Accumulating money can be like a fortress to these folks, a castle that protects them against life's sieges.

Other people are restless. They want something more than they have. For them, money represents the ability to pursue happiness. If they have enough money, they can chase whatever dreams have captured their imaginations. Many times when they arrive at their destination, the dreams seem made of gossamer. This fact might be disappointing for a little while. But then a new idea strikes them and, if they have enough money, they're off again.

For other people, money represents *power*. This is one aspect of money that seems to affect all of us. Even way back in the early church, people struggled with this aspect of money. Why else would James write in the second chapter of his New Testament letter that church members should not show special attention to the guy who walks in with a gold ring, while making the shabbily dressed person sit on the floor? (See James 2:2-4.) We stand in awe of those who have a lot of money and of what they can buy. We yield them power.

And those who have it are not unaffected by our awe of them. Having money can make people feel different from those who don't. If you don't have a lot of money, it's easy to see only the "up" side of that situation. Think of being pampered on vacations, treated well in exclusive shops, having the best table at a restaurant reserved for you.

The Down Side

But there are "down" sides that may not be as visible. For example, when a person has a lot of money, it's easy for her to wonder if she has value to others apart from that money. Would people think she was just as charming if she only had income from a minimum-wage job? Or are they only her friends because they want something from her?

And can someone who has a lot of money trust what others tell him? What about the man asking whether his driver would like to stop for a snack before heading home. What's the driver supposed to say—"No thanks, I'm only here because you pay me"? Won't the driver tell his boss he'd be happy to keep him company, whether or not the driver really wants to? And the rich man knows this at some level.

Further, those who possess a great deal also know fears that many others don't. The writer of Proverbs reflected, "Wealth is a ransom for a person's life, but the poor get no threats" (Prov. 13:8, NRSV). Where do those who have a lot of money find closeness in a culture that worships money as a god, a culture that can make those who have a lot of it feel isolated from real interactions?

It is this other aspect of money—not the economic system of exchange we discussed first, but what might be termed the spiritual nature of money—that causes the most problems.

When someone robs another person of money, the robber does not want to take the money home to put it under the bed. The thief is not threatening another person merely to possess that individual's pieces of paper. The robber wants a shortcut to meeting some need, or probably more accurately, to fulfilling some possibility that the robber thinks money can achieve.

Those of us who struggle along day by day also want money, but we're willing to delay our gratification. We don't take illegal shortcuts, perhaps because of righteousness instilled by faith in God. Or perhaps it's from a fear of getting caught. In any case, we still spend our energies in accumulating and managing money. And we're willing to go to great lengths to get more of it.

Money is important to people. As French historian and sociologist Jacques Ellul has described, two countries once tried to do away with money. But neither could do it. Both China and Cuba eliminated money as a means of exchange for a while, but the experiment failed (Ellul, 1984, pp. 167-168). Today, money is used for exchange and can even be saved in those countries.

We might as well admit it. We human beings like money. Is that really so bad? Can't we do good things as well as terrible things with our money?

As a next step before you begin your personal journey, let's take a look at money from a spiritual point of view.

CHAPTER 2

Spiritual Dynamics

The fact is, we're probably going to have to deal with money as long as we're alive. What we need to do then, as people of faith, is to consider what our attitude might be toward it.

Money is certainly an important topic in the Bible. By one measure, there are more verses about our attitudes toward our material possessions than about prayer, love, or believing.

More specifically, Jesus emphasizes the importance of money in Matthew 6:24. There he says that people who follow him have a choice to make. And he narrows down the choice to only two possibilities. People can serve God or people can serve money.

Why only these two choices? Jacques Ellul made the point that Jesus seems to be telling us something very key in this verse. Money is not just pieces of paper. Money is also a power that is asking for our service and loyalty.

Another way of looking at Matthew 6:24 is to say that there will be one top priority in our lives. In a pinch, we will let that priority decide the matter at hand. We can try all we like to maintain a balance. Eventually, however, we will come down on one side or the other, playing by one set of rules or another.

When we understand the truth of Jesus' statement in Matthew 6:24, then we realize that our attitude toward our money is very important indeed. Money can be a tool for good, or money can be a god. The only difference between the words "good" and "god" is one "o," but the two words represent a world of difference. The decision we make about whose rules we accept will affect every part of our lives.

At this point in our conversation, we especially need to emphasize that money can be a tool for good. One way we get all confused about money is to surround it with guilt. If we won't love it outright, we are often confused about it. We try to resist its attractions and then feel guilty that we have to wrestle with our feelings so much. Whether we love it or resist it, either way we spend a lot of time thinking about money. Rather than being in a struggle with money, we ought to experience the freedom that Jesus Christ promises to give us. Some people suggest that the only way to be free around money is to reject it. But rather than rejecting it, the freedom we have as a result of our faith ought to help us put money in its proper perspective.

A Great Good

When money is good, it can be very good. Money provides us a place to live, food to eat, and clothes to wear. Money provides our family not only with these basic needs, but also with education and preventive health care. On a larger scale, money has been used to send missionaries, translate Bibles, build universities and medical schools, train doctors and teachers, and find cures for diseases.

When our attitudes are right, money can be a positive factor in our worship of God as well. When we were visiting a church in Shanghai, we were told about a poor elderly woman who was a member there. "Wu Ling" moved from a rural area to this large city on the east coast of China to live with her grown children. Wu Ling had become a Christian early in her life and had stayed loyal to her faith during the terrible years of the Cultural Revolution, when religion was banned in China. Now she was free to go to church to attend worship services. However, Wu Ling had no money for the offering. Her son offered to give her money that she could take to church. But like King David who would not offer sacrifices to the Lord that cost him nothing (2 Sam. 24:24), Wu Ling would not take her son's money for the offering at church. She would only make an offering that was the fruit of her own labor. However, she did ask her son for a loan.

Wu Ling took this money to the market and bought some sturdy cotton cloth. Then she layered the material until it was thick. Next, she cut the material into the shape of shoes. Finally, she painfully drew her needle and thread through each thick cushion. When she was done, she had made linings for cotton shoes, such as the Chinese wear to keep their feet warm in the winter.

She then took a small stool down to the open-air market and, sitting in the cold, offered her shoe pads for sale. When she had sold them, she first paid back the loan to her son. Next, she kept enough money to buy more cloth to make more pads. The balance of the money she took to church as her offering to the Lord.

Money can be a tool for great good, if our hearts are in order.

The strange thing is, there are very few places for us to go to put our hearts in order. In a society that is so preoccupied with money, we actually talk very little about what it means to us in any real way.

But What Does It Mean?

Certainly, we talk *about* money. A cynical song in the musical *Cabaret* announced, "Money makes the world go around!" In the 1990s hit movie *Jerry Maguire*, the recurring theme was "Show me the money!" We talk about what money will buy, what it can do, and what bills it will pay. But we don't usually talk about what money means to us.

Even at church we are strangely silent on the topic. Finance committee meetings will go on for hours about what line items to cut, or how to manage a particular debt, or which mission to keep and which to end based on how much was donated last year. But even at church, we don't talk about our loyalties, and our attitudes, about our hopes and fears that are so interwoven with our money.

In a conversation with one young woman, the topic of children's birthday parties came up. The young mother and her husband were feeling the usual pressure to have elaborate parties for their children. Their kids were invited to these events, and so the couple felt they had to respond in kind. However, she and her husband had come up with a unique plan. They would provide the kinds of birthday parties that their children expected. However, this couple decided they would also donate a like amount of money to world missions through their church. When praised for her commitment, the young mother sounded sad. "We're doing this, but it's hard to know if what we're doing is right. It would be so nice to have a group of people to talk with about these issues related to money. I talk with my friends sometimes. But what I would really like is a group at my church."

It might seem natural that such discussions would take place at church. That's where we share the same faith, same Lord, same communion table. We might assume that here we would be able to work through our struggles about money. If the whole area of how we related to our material possessions was so important that God talked about it in over 2,000 verses throughout the Bible, doesn't it seem like it would be important enough for us to talk about with other church members?

But such conversations are not natural. Instead of being free to talk about it, we treat money as if it were a sacred subject that we avoid addressing directly. We dodge the key issue of what money means to us and how we relate to it and to God.

That's why you are to be congratulated. By reflecting on the topics that begin in chapter 5, you are taking a very important step in your spiritual growth. You are opening yourself to exciting possibilities as you rethink your relationship with God and how that relationship affects the way you think about the role that money plays in your life. New freedom can result. And new possibilities.

Chapter 4, on how to use this book, suggests that it can be a private reflection tool or the basis for gathering in a small group. Therefore, we want to give you a brief overview of the purpose of small groups as you consider how to proceed.

CHAPTER 3

The Purpose of Small Groups

Evelyn Freelin wrote what might be termed "an ode to small towns." She cited various examples of "you know you are in a small town when . . ." Her examples range from "Third Street is on the edge of town" to "you were born on June 13 and your family received gifts from the local merchants because you were the first baby of the year." You can tell the advantages of a small town when "you dial a wrong number and talk for 15 minutes anyway." And how about, "You don't use your turn signal because everyone knows where you're going."

Sure, there are disadvantages to small towns where everyone knows your business, but there's a growing sense that we've also lost something when we moved to the anonymity that comes with crowded urban centers. Consider that upscale neighborhoods are building porches on new houses because, in contrast to the more inwardly focused 1980s, there is a trend among people to want more traditional contact with their neighbors. And why else would the refrain from the classic TV show *Cheers* describe the bar as the place "Where everybody knows your name"?

As human beings, we have a hunger to be known. If more and more of us are going to live in urban settings, we're also going to have to figure out how to produce new patterns that meet that need. For many, a small group, or a combination of small groups, fills the bill.

You may be involved in some form of a small group already. Sometimes you might not apply the formal name of "small group" to a set of people you relate to. Are you on a "team" at work that breaks up your department into smaller units? Do you participate in scouting or youth sports, where the larger group is divided into "packs" or teams? Or do you serve on church or school committees where you gather with a group of people for a common purpose? Do you attend a class or reading group or pursue some other activity that brings people together around a common interest? We've visited a number of churches where the "Young Adults" Sunday school class has eventually had to come up with another name. This happened because the group wanted to stay together, even though all of them are now over 50. There's a small group that bonded!

Small group activities undergird how we conduct life in these United States. A group we join may have an external purpose such as planning a special event, or a more internal focus such as sustaining an interest in music. However, for a variety of reasons we organize our-selves so that we come into contact with other people and can exchange ideas with them.

Small groups can also be organized for the specific purpose of helping individuals grow spiritually. This is the type of activity often connected with churches. And it is this type of group we recommend to you as you journey on the path to exploring your relationship with God and money.

You may be ready right now to form a small group and begin to use the topics presented in chapters 5 through 7. It's very possible that you have extensive small group experience, given how many people in the United States already participate in this kind of activity. If that is the case, you should feel free to turn now to chapter 10 and review the guide provided for organizing such a group. This information may confirm your own experiences or provide some helpful additional insights that can help you launch a successful small group that considers how people relate to God and money.

However, you should note that talking about money is a particularly difficult challenge in our culture. People don't usually discuss financial matters in a personal way. So, if you have not had a lot of small group experience, or even if you have, we have provided some information in this chapter, as well as in chapters 8 and 9, that you might find helpful as a foundation on which to build.

Of course, it's not just talking about money that makes organizing a successful small group a special kind of task. Human beings, being what we are, find conducting an effective small group to be a challenge, no matter what the stated topic. Giving you some additional background about small groups is a way to provide you with a feeling of confidence as you use the topics in this book to talk with others about faith and money in a small group.

Right now we want to reflect a little about the purpose of small groups. Here we consider why people join small groups, and some of the roles these gatherings play in our lives.

Then, after you've had a chance to read through the topics, you'll find a brief history of small groups presented in chapter 8. You will see that you are participating in a grand tradition that has strengthened the church throughout many years.

It's in chapter 9 that we provide some tips on how to run an effective small group. We explore various aspects of organizing a small group —from the invitation, to the role of the leader, to some behaviors that you might want to be prepared to deal with—as you and others gather to explore your feelings about God and money.

Finally, in chapter 10, a step-by-step guide shows you how a small group might be organized.

If people are willing to open up, a small group on faith and money can be a positive experience for all those involved. These chapters are designed to help you and those you are traveling with on this journey of discovery to have the best experience possible.

Moving Toward Wholeness

Back in 1992 a cartoon in *The New Yorker* showed two dogs relaxing. The one with a sad face observed, "I've got the bowl, the bone, the big yard. I know I *should* be happy..."

As humans, we keep learning and relearning that it takes more than possessions to meet our emotional needs. One key element in our lives seems to be human interaction. If we don't come by it naturally, we tend to organize ourselves into it. And the form that our organization often takes is to develop some kind of small group.

Take churches, for example. Churches have a lot of small groups: Sunday school classes, committees, Bible studies, youth group, women's circles, men's fellowship. The goal of these groups is generally to make the larger community of faith have a more personal meaning for its members. There are also civic organizations, reading clubs, music societies, and therapy and self-help groups that may meet in churches, but have no formal relationship with them. In our present discussion, we are particularly interested in the small group of people that gathers to pursue the spiritual growth of the participants.

Renewed relationships. Gareth Icenogle, a pastor and professor who teaches about small groups, has studied and implemented small groups. He thinks they have the potential for impacting the world around us in a positive way. In his book, *Biblical Foundations for Small Group Ministry*, he writes:

> The stewardship of creation is the responsibility of human com-
> munity. Small groups are base camps for the stewardship of
> creation. Creation ministry rolls out of the health of human re-
> lationships. Unhealthy or "dysfunctional" human community un-
> leashes its destructive forces on creation" (Icenogle, 1994, p. 24).

In other words, if small groups can help us to move closer to God and relate to each other more as God intends, then it is likely there will be a positive overflow into world conditions around us.

This is a particularly intriguing idea as we consider a small group that is especially focused on our relationships to God and to money. When we deal with money, as we've talked about in earlier chapters, we are dealing with a spiritual power. If we're not handling it in a way that fits in with our faith, it seems likely that our individual problems will combine with those of others to have a negative effect on the world around us. If we do not approach money with the kind of transformed mind that Paul writes about in Romans 12:2, then we may create prob-lems, not only for ourselves, but on a larger scale as well. Don't forget that Paul also wrote that "the love of money is a root of all kinds of evil" (1 Tim. 6:10 NRSV).

Building on Icenogle's idea, a small group that helps us think through our attitudes toward money in light of our faith in Jesus Christ can serve as a "base camp" for a renewed relationship, not only with other people, but also with God's creation around us.

Perspective in a confusing world. While the goal is to move toward wholeness in God, the transformation process is not easy in a world that seems to be going in another direction. In *"I Come Away Stronger": How Small Groups Are Shaping American Religion*, Robert Wuthnow, the director of the Center for the Study of American Religion at Princeton University, presents case studies of small groups in religious life. Re-flecting on his findings, he writes:

Many Americans feel pressured by advertising and by their
employers and by a myriad of other cultural influences to live
in ways that pay little attention to questions of spirituality.
Some are finding the support to resist these pressures in small
groups (Wuthnow, 1994a, p. 345).

There is a general consensus among experts that the support structures people once relied on are no longer available to most Americans.
People do not have extended families living close to them. It's very
common to change jobs many times during a career and, as a result, not
build long-term loyalties. People may not go to church, shop, or even go
to school in their own neighborhood.

Howard Snyder is professor of history and theology of mission at
Asbury Seminary. In *The Problem of Wineskins* he describes the situation in these terms:

Modern technopolis is a different world. Thanks in part to
urban mobility, we live in several distinct worlds in the course
of a week: office, shop, neighborhood, school, club. The church
is only one world among others for the majority of Americans
(Snyder, 1975, p. 144).

In an academic book on the role of small groups in therapy called
Encounter: Group Processes for Interpersonal Growth, psychologist
Gerard Egan points out that the isolation resulting from the lack of support structures makes many people dependent on the one-way communication of television or movies. He cites a study that suggests people face
real difficulty in our culture because (1) many people find little emotional satisfaction in their work, and (2) they do not interact on a familiar level with different people as they did when surrounded by close
relatives and longtime neighbors. Egan suggests that it is important for
people therefore to structure contacts with other people to obtain "emotional fulfillment" (Egan, 1970, pp. 144-145).

So, small groups have a key part to play in our modern culture.
They allow us to interact with people on a deeper level than we usually
have the opportunity to do. In particular, in a society in which we do not
normally talk about how we feel about money, a small group can be an
ideal setting in which to develop and encourage healthy attitudes that
are consistent with our faith.

Relating to God and people. Icenogle develops some very interesting ideas about the theological aspects of small groups. He notes that, in one real sense, the Trinity itself—of Father, Son, and Holy Spirit—can be seen as "community," another way of describing a small group. Further, the impulse in creation was to develop a community between God and two human beings. When that community was broken apart, Jesus Christ then came to restore the possibility of community between God and people once more (Icenogle, 1994, pp. 12, 21).

So gathering together with other Christians to explore how to become more whole in Jesus Christ can be said to be very much in keeping with God's plan.

What to expect. We should be careful about the expectations we bring to such a group, however. Wuthnow conducted a national survey on small groups. He reports his findings in *Sharing the Journey: Support Groups and America's New Quest for Community*. As he has rightly pointed out, the small groups of today do not usually replace our extended families as an even exchange. For one thing, many of us bring late twentieth-century attitudes to our agreements to participate in such a group (Wuthnow, 1994b, pp. 6, 12). If we decide we don't like a small group, we may choose to withdraw.

Such is not the case with family. Of course, there are days when we could all agree with George Burns' observation, "Happiness is having a large, loving, caring, close-knit family—in another city." Still, for many, family means not only that we have to put up with *them*, but they have to put up with *us*. There are deep ties in family. Many say this basic structure in our society is weakening. But near or far, the level of commitment to and responsibility for family is deeply ingrained in most of us.

In contrast, we can move in and out of small groups, as many Americans do. We need to make a conscious decision to stay committed to a voluntary small group through the ups and downs of the relationship. It is a choice not to run at the first sign of disagreement.

Many choose to make this commitment because small groups can meet very real needs. Wuthnow reports that 82 percent of those participating in a small group agreed that the group "Made you feel like you weren't alone" and 72 percent agreed that the group "Gave you encouragement when you were feeling down." Groups can encourage participants, he says, as well as provide advice and provide what is described in church circles as fellowship (Wuthnow, 1994b, pp. 170-171).

The danger of self-centeredness. People who either study or lead small groups often raise one serious concern related to groups. That is, it is too easy for a group to become so comfortable that it becomes self-centered. In particular, for those who join a group to get to know God better, it is a very serious problem if the participants turn completely inward. In such a case, they can no longer be described as seeking to be strengthened in order to reach out to others as a result of their interactions with those in the group.

For example, one man quoted by Wuthnow wondered if many small groups were "making people feel better about themselves but were not necessarily motivating them to be better people" (Wuthnow, 1994b, p. 188).

Icenogle also warns of a group too occupied with its own needs: "Too often small groups have a reputation for being caring and supportive of one another but having no positive impact on the way people behave toward creation or the world beyond" (Icenogle, 1994, p. 24).

Clyde Reid wrote *Groups Alive—Church Alive* in 1969, as the small group movement was expanding. His experience with small groups came as a staff member at the Institute for Advanced Pastoral Studies in Bloomfield, Michigan. He also worked with small groups at Union Theological Seminary in New York. Reid goes so far as to say, "When a group becomes centered on itself, this may be one indication its usefulness has ceased" (Reid, 1969, p. 103).

But wait a minute! Haven't we been making a big deal about how important it is to explore our own individual attitudes based on our own personal experiences? How can you avoid having a self-centered group when the whole focus is on such a personal topic as our attitudes toward money?

There may not be as much conflict between these two goals as it might at first appear. In order to come to terms with the power of money in our lives and to bring that power in submission to our relationship with God, we will indeed have to do some very personal soul-searching. And we continue to recommend that you be in the company of a few trusted companions on this journey of personal discovery.

Perhaps the difference between an ingrown group and a growing group is where the participants are headed. Do you gather regularly just to pat each other on the back and reassure each other that nothing's really that wrong after all? Or do you come together to encourage each other, to strengthen those things that are worth keeping, and also to change those things you might be better off without?

The guide in the last chapter suggests an occasional reflection question for your group to consider about its progress. You may find these questions very helpful in figuring out if you've begun to grow moss or if you're still rolling toward increased faithfulness.

Summary. Small groups are a form of community in this currently dislocated society. They can provide encouragement, fulfill our need for human interaction at a more than superficial level, and help us figure out how best to proceed in various areas of our lives.

Small groups seem to have a role within the faith community, in particular. We are each working to be in a better relationship to God and our neighbors. The chance to step back and reflect on how best to go about that is a valuable service that small groups can perform.

However, the very process of gathering with others on a regular basis can meet a need for emotional interaction which can then remove our appetite for growth. So as we gather to reflect on the role of money and faith in our lives, we need to keep our eye on the larger goal of why we began the discussion in the first place.

The topics presented in this book are designed to help you grow both inwardly and outwardly. The next chapter discusses how you can make the best use of these discussion questions in your individual journey.

CHAPTER 4

How to Use This Book

There's the story of the pastor who asked if anyone in the congregation needed prayer. One troubled looking man rose from his seat. "Reverend," he said, "I have to confess that I'm a terrible spendthrift. I spend money like it was water. Reverend, I need your prayers." The minister smiled kindly and announced, "Friends, let's pray for this gentleman. But first, I think it's time for the offering!"

One reason people may have trouble sharing their feelings about money in church is because they feel that the church wants their money. Let's be frank. Of course the church wants money. It takes money to operate the activities of the congregation, and more money besides to take initiative on sharing God's love in word and deed with a hurting world. And one way the church obtains money is to ask for it.

However, let's also be very clear about an important point. As much as it is reasonable for the church to want people to be good givers, that is not what this book is about. Improving giving levels, while a worthy goal, is not the topic at hand. The reflection experiences in this book are designed for a very different purpose. It's vital that you and everyone who reads this book understand that point from the beginning.

In fact, it's not clear what will happen to people as a result of thinking about the issues raised on the following pages. A particular person may or may not change his giving habits, or her spending habits, or even their attitudes about some aspects of money. All these are important parts of loving God. But no particular results are guaranteed for those using this book. There are no right answers or expected results defined by the experience of thinking through how you feel about God and money. It would not really be an adventure if we had a road map all laid out, with prerecorded tourist monologues describing the sights you will see at each point.

No, the reflections that result from going through this book will be a disappointment to anyone who starts out with fixed expectations of where other people should end up in order for the experience to be successful. Rather, the goal is for the reader—for you—to feel secure enough to think through some important ideas, and then to see what happens.

How the Book Is Organized

There are three levels of questions presented on the following pages. The sets of questions are designed to help you move from introductory topics toward progressively deeper issues related to discipleship. Within each level, there are three clusters, or sets, of 15 questions. Again, each cluster moves the reader further on the road of discovery (see diagram on following page).

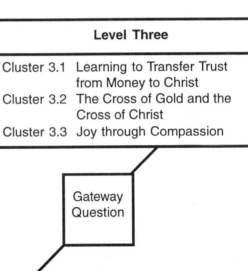

The first level can be summarized by the general question, "How Are We Supposed to Think about Money?" The three clusters within this level begin with introductory topics, then explore how our attitudes were originally formed about money, and, lastly, examine patterns we have developed in the way we think about money.

At the end of the third cluster of topics within this first level, there is what we call a Gateway Question. This question helps you decide if you are ready to go to the next level of topics or not. If not, you might want to return to particular questions that you found especially interesting in level 1. You can reconsider moving to the next level at some point in the future.

The second level is summarized by the description, "Practical Issues of Stewardship and Budgeting." Here in level 2, the first cluster of 15 questions explores issues in budgeting—but not from a dollar and cents point of view! You then move to topics on "Trimming, Pruning, Firming." The last cluster in level 2 discusses what Jesus had to say about money.

Once again, you can use the second Gateway Question to decide if you want to move to level three.

The third level explores issues having to do with discipleship. The first cluster of topics in level 3 looks at the issue of how we transfer trust from money to Christ. The second cluster leads you through a consideration of what role self-discipline and self-denial might play in our self-indulgent world. Finally, the last section talks about the joys and freedom that are to be found in harnessing the power of money through the power of Christ.

You may choose to begin at level 1, cluster 1, question 1, and proceed to level 1, cluster 1, question 2, etc. This pattern might be followed all the way through question 15 in the third cluster of level 3 if you like.

Another approach is to select the questions within a cluster at random, like selecting one grape out of a bunch. You can write the numbers 1 through 15 on slips of paper and then select a slip for each session.

You might also choose to consider only some of the topics in a particular cluster and move quickly to the next cluster without using all the topics in the previous one before you leave it. If, at a later point, you decide you do not want to move to the next level, perhaps you will want to come back and pick up any questions that were not considered the first time through.

The key point to understand is that the topics offered on these pages are designed to spur your thinking about important ideas in fresh ways. You should be challenged, but also you should enjoy yourself during the process. You will be the best judge of how to work through the questions, based on the situation you find yourself in at the point you read this book.

To proceed from here, however, you do have one choice to make. You can use this book as a tool for individual reflection only. Or, you can join together with a small group of people who are also interested in going on this journey of discovery.

A Journey of Private Reflection

This book can be used on an individual basis. The best way to proceed on your own might be to use the topics in this book as part of a journaling experience.

The journal would be used to record your observations and thoughts about a particular idea or question presented on the following pages. It can be a formal leather-bound book, or a three-hole binder or folder filled with a supply of lined paper. You can use one or more pages in your journal for each topic, or you can write on one topic and then continue the next on the same page, after skipping a line.

You will probably want to date each entry. Looking back later, you might wonder what was going on in your life when you wrote a particular observation, and the dates can help you keep your own history clear.

Your goal should be to write as honestly and freely as possible. There will be no one grading your paper! You are trying to think through these ideas. Find a writing style that is comfortable for you, and then use it to help you consider the issues that are raised.

You will probably have more success if you set aside some time on a regular basis to do this journaling. You will be the best judge about what pattern works best for you. Is there a particular day of the week when you can set aside a few minutes to be alone, to think and reflect? Or is having a regular time at the beginning or end of each day better for you?

Will you stay on the same topic from day to day for a week, or even from week to week for a month, or will you start a new idea each time?

You might find yourself using a combination of these two ideas. You might stay with one topic during several reflection times because you find it a particularly fruitful vein of thought. Or you might find that a single session is sufficient to cover another topic.

However, don't try to cram several topics into one session. Give thoughtful attention to one idea each time. This type of slow reflection will be helpful to you as you explore your thinking.

You might also want to reread the Litany presented at the front of this book on a regular basis. Using a short reflective prayer can help you to focus your thoughts as you consider these ideas.

The purpose of your journaling is to explore your feelings in the context of your faith. The issues raised in the various clusters are designed to guide you in this process. While you are not looking for a specific result, the overall goal is for you to move to a new freedom in how you approach the topic of God and money in your life.

Traveling Together in a Small Group

Gathering a group of people together to reflect on these topics is another way to use this book. The participants might want to keep private, individual journals in which to write their feelings about the topic that is going to be discussed at the next group meeting. On the other hand, they might not. In either case, it is a good idea to preselect the topic that is going to be discussed the next time the group meets. In that way, people can be thinking ahead about some aspects of the issue that will be discussed, resulting in a richer level of participation during the next discussion.

The topics also may be used in previously established groups. You might want to set aside 15 minutes at the start of your church council meeting or at the beginning of the finance committee agenda. Stepping back to reflect on some spiritual aspect of money might be very useful for a group that regularly meets to conduct the "business" of the church.

You might also want to organize a more intentional effort to help those involved grow into a deeper understanding of their relationships to God and money. The point of an intentional small group organized specifically to talk about the topics in this book is to set up a "safe zone" in a world fraught with confusion and danger about the topic of money. In the small group that gathers to talk about these issues, it should be understood from the beginning that there are no "right" or "wrong" answers. Any attitude that is voiced is true in the sense that the person saying it feels that way. As a result, ideas will be exchanged, and those sharing may change their opinions over time, or they may not. It's important that there is no pressure on anyone to conform to a particular way of thinking. Each person is on a journey to know himself or herself better, and to know God better. Each will travel at an individual pace. The goal of the group should be to make each person feel free to enjoy the trip as much as possible.

That does not mean that the group should not honestly interact with each other. To not be honest with each other would be a waste of everyone's time. What it does mean is that people can share their opinions and responses to others' comments by acknowledging that these views come from their own perspectives, rather than stating that these views are the only right way to think about a topic.

As a participant in the group, you should feel free to reveal as much of yourself to the others present as you care to, but no more. You might feel that you can talk quite freely about a topic one week, and then the next week not want to talk much at all. Each person in the group should be given the opportunity to talk, but not be pressured to talk more than he or she wants to.

When you do feel free to talk, you'll also want to be careful to leave room for others who might have to work a little more at sharing that particular week. Don't be afraid of silence. Sometimes everyone should be free to spend a little time with his or her own thoughts before the group goes on with the discussion.

A chapter at the end of this book provides a specific outline of how an intentional small group might be organized. The litany that is included at the front of this book can be read at the beginning of each meeting to remind the participants of the overarching purpose of the discussion.

And We're Off!

These first few chapters have provided you with some background information and preparation for the journey. However, the time has come to shove away from the dock, throw off the towlines, and head out to open sea. Remember Jesus' promise to be with us always (Matt. 28:20). You are in good hands, so relax and enjoy the journey. Bon voyage!

PART 2

Topics for Consideration

CHAPTER 5

Level 1 Overview

How Are We Supposed to Think about Money

If you had been an ancient Egyptian, you would have used onions and beans for your money. Why, imagine—when we sit down to a steaming bowl of chili on a cold winter night, we might be gobbling down the cost of a new chariot!

It's possible the cold of Siberia affected the nasal passages of the folks who lived there years ago. Otherwise, how do you explain that they chose garlic as their medium of exchange?

And do you know what some primitive societies used for money? Beetle legs. What do you think, would that make you into a bug lover or an expert dissector?

It just goes to prove the garage-sale adage that one person's junk is another person's treasure. We are also reminded that we are generally taught what to value by the culture we live in.

Our education about values takes place in smaller units, too. Early on, we learn what we should consider to be important by watching what the members of our families do, as well as what they say.

Sometimes these attitudes are so deeply instilled in us that it doesn't occur to us that they are opinions. We think of them as absolutes.

That can be all right if the attitudes are working in our favor. Certain values tend to produce good results all the time. At least nine times out of ten, your boss is going to appreciate the fact that you are a hard worker who shows up on time. Honesty saves you the trouble of keeping all your stories straight. These are values that continue to reinforce themselves.

But there are signs that our attitudes toward money may not always be helpful. For example, consider the fact that while we have more and more things, polls show we see fewer friends regularly. Is this an improvement?

This is your chance to consider which attitudes about money you want to keep and which you want to change. But in order to do that, we need to take a fresh look at some very familiar ideas.

Sometimes it's hard to even know that we are culture-bound in our attitudes toward money. We realized firsthand how much we'd been influenced by our backgrounds when we lived in the People's Republic of China for a year.

For one thing, at that time in the mid-1980s, relationships in China often carried more value than money. This was a very strange idea for those of us who came from the consumer-oriented United States! You could have the correct amount of *yuan* (Chinese currency) to buy a product. However, if, for example, the clerk thought that her boss might possibly be interested in the item for his nephew, and if the item was in limited supply, no amount of money would convince her to sell it to you. From her point of view, you were just passing through, but her boss affected every part of her life, from her housing arrangements to which hours she worked. Your money would go into the government company's coffers. Keeping her boss's nephew happy could make the circumstances of her life improve.

We had a more direct culture clash over how people view earnings. In China it was not considered at all rude to ask a perfect stranger both his age and his income. For us Americans, the first time we understood the question, the reply got stuck in our throats. We had to make a conscious effort to choose to answer the question. Calming our racing hearts, we provided the information. Initially, the conversation ended there, because it didn't occur to us to ask the same question back. However, the second and third time it happened, the shock was a little less. And do you know, we were actually interested to hear what the other person told us in reply. In fact, we learned some fascinating information when people told us about the details of their lives.

No doubt, things have changed in China in the intervening years. As private enterprise has become more of a possibility, personal income may also have become more private. But our encounters with a different culture showed us that these deeply ingrained attitudes about the privacy of money were opinions, not laws. Sometimes it's good to sit back and look at ideas that seem very firmly set. Every so often, we need to ask ourselves if understandings that we take for granted are indeed true, or even useful. That's what this first level of topics is designed to help you do as you think about the spiritual nature of money.

Cluster 1 presents 15 topics we have labeled "Introductory." They might also be called warm-up questions. Because we don't usually talk about how we feel about money, it takes some practice to cozy up to the idea. These questions are designed to help you get your toes wet, knowing that you are still in the wading pool.

Cluster 2 also includes 15 questions. These topics take us in a slightly more personal direction. Here, we talk about how we first learned our attitudes toward money. How was money talked about in our homes? Who were our role models? Spending a little time exploring these issues will help you lay the groundwork for further discussions as we go on.

Then cluster 3 considers our individual money habits. One of us jokes that she did not receive the "shopping gene" that her sisters seem to have inherited. But, of course, the way we spend or save money is far more the result of how we were brought up than the DNA in our bodies. We can have deeply set habits that lead us to handle money in a certain way. In these 15 questions, you have a chance to take a look at some of your own patterns, perhaps from a different perspective. You might find that you want to encourage certain habits. Others may give you pause, as you begin to refine how you want to relate to God and money in your life.

The Gateway Question between level 1 and level 2 should be considered seriously before moving on. This journey of faith is on a completely voluntary basis. Therefore, you will want to figure out what you want to do before you leave the first level behind.

The road lies before you. Ready? Then let's begin.

Cluster 1.1

Learning to Float

French writer Marcel Proust once observed, "People wish to learn to swim and at the same time to keep one foot on the ground." At some point, of course, we have to trust ourselves to the water if we are to master the technique needed to keep us from sinking.

But most of us who learned to swim did not just jump into deep water. The first stage was to become comfortable at a depth where we felt safe. And the first goal was probably to learn to float. If you had a really good instructor, that person told you that your body will work with you to keep you afloat. The air in your lungs will make it hard for you to sink unless a great weight pulls you down. So the key to floating is to relax and to trust.

In the same way, these first 15 questions are designed to help you become a little more comfortable with the topic of money. Select one for each session and give yourself enough time to really think about the ideas involved. We assure you, it's natural to float. So, just relax and enjoy!

1. What did I buy this week? How did I decide to buy it?

2. What was the best commercial I saw in the last week, and how did it make me feel?

3. If I were to share one thing about me and money with someone else, what would it be?

4. What temptation have I had in buying/spending this week? What was my response?

5. What dreams do I have which I think money protects for me?

6. What is the last possession I would want to give up?

7. What possessions would I forgo purchasing if God asked me to?

8. How is my sense of safety or security tied up with money?

9. Would I feel less valued if I had less money, or more valued if I had more money? Why?

10. How do I feel about me, God, and money this week?

11. How are wealth and authentic devotion to God related?

12. What did I buy in the last year or two that cost between $100 and $1,000? What pressures or influences was I aware of in the process of making a decision to buy?

13. What is my definition for "mad money" or "found money"? What rules, if any, govern the way I spend such money?

14. How can salvation at the same time be free and yet cost everything I have?

15. Jesus says I will be happier in giving than in receiving. Is this always true? In what ways does this seem to be true and in which ways does it not?

End of cluster 1.1.
Go on to cluster 1.2.

Cluster 1.2

Where Did We Learn This Stuff?

According to humorist Dennis Fakes, "Any child can tell you that the sole purpose of a middle name is so he can tell when he's really in trouble." What each of us got in trouble for differed from family to family, and even from child to child within the same family. What we got in trouble for often helped us to understand what our families considered important. Our families, combined with community, church, and school, had a major impact on forming our values. As we continue to grow, we sort out for ourselves where we agree and disagree with what we've been taught.

This next set of questions is designed to guide you through discussions about how some of your basic attitudes toward money were formed. But don't worry. Nobody will call you by your middle name as you explore your feelings!

1. How was money discussed in my parental home?

2. With whom am I most comfortable speaking about money? Why?

3. Do persons become more or less generous as they grow older?

4. When in my life have I been least concerned about money? Why then?

5. When in my life have I been most concerned about money? Why then?

6. Who is the most generous person I know? How has that person expressed his or her generosity?

7. "Miser" in Latin means a wretch or *miserable* person. Do I know any person for whom stinginess has meant wretchedness? What do I learn from that?

8. What single act in the life of Jesus most impresses me as generous?

9. The root word of "generous" means "according to kind" ("kindly") or "natural." Is generosity natural?

10. What are one or two of the most generous acts of which I have been the recipient? What was my response and why?

11. When has God allowed me to practice an act of unusual kindness? What were the results and why?

12. What person do I most admire for his or her expertise, ingenuity, or creativity in handling money? What have I learned from that person?

13. Is shrewdness or good business sense compatible with generosity?

14. How have my attitudes about money changed in the last year or two?

15. When I am honest with myself, I recognize that my main problem with money is _____.

End of cluster 1.2.
Go on to cluster 1.3.

Cluster 1.3

Habits or Addictions?

Have you ever bitten your fingernails, or known someone who did? It produces ugly results, doesn't it? It's also a hard habit to break.

One of us struggled with this bad habit for years. And what does the biter get for it? Craggy nails, snagged stockings, and embarrassment when extending a hand on first meeting someone. So why do it? Like many negative behaviors, it met some strong need that conquered the will to do differently. What's the solution? To meet an even stronger positive force that helps us redefine what our needs are. That happened for the nail biter among us during high school.

The apostle Paul describes his own experience with compelling behaviors in his letter to the Romans. There's nothing to indicate he was a nail biter, but he had obviously struggled with the same kind of forces. He wrote, "I do not understand what I do. For what I want to do I do not do, but what I hate I do" (Rom. 7:15 NIV). But the story does not end there. We struggle, but we can also win. Paul continued in his letter to the early Roman Christians: "Therefore, there is now no condemnation for those who are in Christ Jesus, because through Christ Jesus the law of the Spirit of life set me free from the law of sin and death" (Rom. 8:1-2 NIV).

Even if we find ingrained habits that define how we relate to money, we don't have to be stuck with them. There is a power stronger than mammon. And the power of the Spirit wants us to be free!

1.   Sociologist Philip Slater in *Wealth Addictions* describes five sorts of wealth addiction. There are, he says, *money addicts* (misers), *possession addicts* (accumulators of things), *power addicts* (those who use money for control), *fame addicts* (those who use money to get glory), and *spending addicts* (those who like to have money to travel, entertain, amuse themselves). Is addiction a useful model for describing these sorts of behavior? Why or why not? For private consideration: What kind of personal expenditures would I be least comfortable discussing in this connection?

2. How can money mean *freedom*, and how can it mean *the loss of freedom*?

3. What I most like about money is _____. What I most fear about money is _____.

4. Is there an area of spending about which God has helped me to be newly conscientious? How did this come about?

5. Are there ways in which I take pleasure in sheer accumulation or collection? How am I keeping this under review?

6. Are there ways in which my church or another group appears to demonstrate a fondness for accumulation? How is this kept under review?

7. Setting aside at least ten percent of income for *savings* is often recommended as wise stewardship. Can saving money be an addictive behavior? Why or why not?

8. *Redundancy* (duplication of components or parts) is vital in space craft and in the human body. (It is less desirable in writing and speaking.) Are there areas of redundancy in my wardrobe, garage, home furnishings? How am I keeping these under review?

9. Something I have purchased in the past year and never or seldom used is _____. Looking back from this distance, what does that purchase tell me?

10. C.S. Lewis has suggested that in hell the reprobates will realize they have spent their lives doing neither what they should have done nor what they truly wanted to do. Have I recently found myself spending money without reflection and without truly wishing to spend it that way? What can I learn from this?

11. What one or two good habits in spending have I developed in the past few years?

12. Though Jesus was constantly talking about money, he seemed quite free of worries about it. How might this be explained?

13. Money itself often serves to pay for addictions of sundry kinds (food, alcohol, sex, etc.). Does money-love actually encourage any of these to develop? How?

14. God is helping me deal with love of money by _____.

15. Do persons who start out with little money find it easier or harder than do others to handle it later in life?

End of cluster 1.3.
Before going on to level 2, take time to reflect on the level 1 Gateway Question on the next page.

Level 1 Gateway Question

Before you go on to level 2, take some time to reflect on the following Gateway Question.

If you feel comfortable with your answer, then go on to level 2 for the next round in your reflection experience.

However, if you feel some reservations about your answer to this question, you might want to go back through a few of the topics in level 1. Perhaps you skipped one the first time through. Or you might consider in more depth some of the earlier questions that challenged you most. Take your time until you are comfortable. Then come back and review this question once again. It will be waiting for you.

Gateway Question for level 1:

Am I willing to make changes in the way I relate to money as I listen to God's voice in my life?

CHAPTER 6

Level 2 Overview

Practical Issues of Stewardship and Budgeting

Could we have thought of a more boring title to summarize level 2? The idea that stewardship and budgeting can be interesting seems a little foreign to most of us. We probably should be interested, but we rarely are.

Even with new computer programs that can produce color charts showing where all the money goes, the idea of creating and following a budget just isn't glamorous. It still comes down to juggling a lot of numbers and probably being disappointed at the resulting totals.

And stewardship! There are leaders in the church today who feel the word has so much baggage that we should find a fresh alternative.

Yet, we hope you'll find the topics on the following pages anything but boring. We are not going to provide you with a step-by-step "how to" or a form to fill out. Just as in level 1, we will offer you some ideas to reflect on.

In this section, we hope you'll be willing to rethink very familiar attitudes. All of us learned to think about money very early in our lives. As a result, it's easy to forget that at some point we had to be introduced to the basic concepts that undergird the economic system we now take for granted.

The following incident reminded us of just how much we learn at different times in our lives. A father was trying to teach his preschool son the value of money and work. So he gave him small jobs to do. In this way, the son could earn some change. Tasks equal to his size would yield a nickel or a dime, if done on a regular basis.

One day the father was sorting the items in his pockets. The contents were spread on the dining room table, including some bills as well as coins. His young son came over and began asking about the bills and their relationship to the coins. Delighted at his son's budding interest in math, the father explained that there were 20 nickels in a dollar, and ten dimes. "When I have ten dimes, can I have a dollar?" the son asked. The father was proud of his son's quick understanding of these sophisticated concepts. "Of course," he replied.

The next week the small boy sought out his father. They sat down at the dining room table together. The son carefully counted out ten dimes. "Now can I have a dollar?" he asked.

The father was beaming. "Of course you can." He pulled out his wallet, took out a dollar bill and handed it to his son. Then our friend began to gather up the ten dimes that sat on the table. His son was alarmed and began trying to grab the dimes first. The father was confused as he said, "But I gave you the dollar." The young boy wailed, "But you said I could have a dollar when I got ten dimes." The problem dawned on the father as his son cried great tears. "The dollar is equal to ten dimes," the father tried to explain. "You can trade the ten dimes for a dollar bill, but you don't get both."

The young boy could not yet understand the very basic idea of exchange. If he had worked hard and saved the dimes, hadn't his good efforts meant that he got the dollar bill *as well*?

This little person learned a basic concept that he would use throughout his life. But sometimes ideas and patterns creep into our behavior that may not be so helpful. On the next pages you will be offered the opportunity to work through a few of the patterns and concepts that you've embraced in your own life. Like a good gardener, you will want to cultivate those that are producing good fruit. And you may want to hoe out those that you find are starting to look like weeds.

In cluster 2.1, the summary topic is "Me and My Budget." Here the questions do not revolve around the right amount to spend on groceries versus utilities, although a good discussion might be had on that very point. Rather, the topics invite you to explore what some of your own spending patterns might mean in a larger context.

The second cluster is summarized as "Trimming, Pruning, Firming." You will be able to tell that we have left level 1 behind when you consider these 15 questions in cluster 2.2. Once again, there are no right or wrong answers, but the issues should provoke an opportunity for some hard thinking.

The final group of questions in level 2 looks at what Jesus had to say about money. Through these 15 topics in cluster 2.3, you are invited to engage in a conversation that has been started by Jesus Christ himself.

As before, when you have completed going through the topics in level 2, give the Gateway Question serious consideration before you move on to level 3. You will be asked to consider whether you are interested in continuing on the path you have begun. If you feel you need a little more time, go back to some of the ideas in level 2 and see how they look after you have been away from them for a few weeks. Give yourself plenty of time to amble at your own pace. And when you are ready, come back to the Gateway Question once more in preparation for moving on to level 3.

We hope you have a delightful time exploring these ideas!

Cluster 2.1

Me and My Budget

Comedian George Burns once noted that it's "too bad that all the people who know how to run the country are busy driving taxicabs and cutting hair."

A distant vantage point makes it easy to give other people advice about their situation. And maybe that's why it's sometimes difficult to figure out what's important and what isn't in our own lives. We're so close to the issues that it's hard to be objective.

In the next 15 questions, you won't be asked to develop a series of line items that define how you spend your money. Rather, let's look at some of the issues that are just under the surface when we make an attempt to organize our personal finances. These topics should help you step back enough to gain that valuable perspective usually reserved for cab drivers and barbers.

1. How am I accountable to at least one other person in how I spend my money?

2. What feature of my personal spending patterns pleases me most, and which the least?

3. If I came into a wholly unexpected $10,000 tomorrow, what would determine the way I used the money?

4. Basically I go shopping in order to _____.

5. How does my personal devotional life relate to my budgeting of money?

6. Coveting is usually understood to mean wanting something that belongs to another. Can it also mean wanting something *just like* what belongs to someone else (car, house, clothes, appliances, gardens, farm equipment, computers, etc.)?

7. Do I often justify purchases by saying I am actually buying them for other people? Am I being realistic in this?

8. A biographer has said that the documents most revealing of a subject's true character are his check stubs. After study of my own check record for the past few months, what do I discover about myself that I had not earlier noticed?

9. Some notable Christians have said that to have a budget is to avoid living by faith. What do I think of this?

10. Should I spend money on total strangers? Why or why not?

11. Should I spend money on people who do not appreciate my investment in them? Why or why not?

12. After a special achievement, do I reward myself with special purchases (e.g., shoes, books, meals out, trips)? How do I keep this under review?

13. Is it easier to budget when I have a little money or a lot of it?

14. The parable of the ten talents (Matt. 25:14-30) suggests that God expects us to take risks with what we are given. How does risk-taking fit with budgeting?

15. What should I do with that occasional startling impulse to simplify my life in some radical way?

End of cluster 2.1.
Go on to cluster 2.2.

Cluster 2.2

Trimming, Pruning, Firming

The only exception to the rule that people don't like rules is in sports. There, people thrive on the goal-tending rule in basketball, the infield pop-fly rule in baseball, or the offsides call in football. It's obvious that any two teams would be competing in chaos if there were not officials to enforce the rules.

Once you leave the sporting field, however, it's a whole 'nother game, so to speak. People don't like rules. They complain of "legalism." Rules, they say, limit creativity.

Yet, there is also a part of us that hungers to know whether we're doing things in the right way or not. The absence of rules leaves a sense of insecurity. How much is okay to spend on a new set of golf clubs? Or is it even okay to have golf clubs? If you asked us, we'd probably say that equipment isn't important. But then, don't tell us how often we should pay to go to the movies. On reflection, maybe it's just as well for each of us to make our own decisions on these particular matters.

And that's largely the point. We have great freedom in Christ. As Paul wrote to the Galatians, "It is for freedom that Christ has set us free" (Gal. 5:1 NIV).

There are general ground rules laid out by the two great commandments that Jesus quotes in Mark 12:29-31: Love God and love your neighbor as yourself. Beyond that, it's largely up to us to figure out the fine points. Our reflections on these matters will probably benefit from a combination of inspiration and creativity. And don't forget, as Ralph Waldo Emerson observed, "Common sense is genius dressed in its working clothes."

Even though we don't have specific rules for every situation, we can still develop healthy guidelines. Have fun in your garden of budgets, as you trim, prune, and firm for greater growth!

1. 1 Timothy 6:8 suggests that I should be content if I have food and clothing. How literally should I take this?

2. For the serious Christian disciple, what is an appropriate entertainment budget?

3. For the serious Christian disciple, what is an appropriate travel budget?

4. For the serious Christian disciple, what is appropriate support for artists of all kinds?

5. Statistics indicate that Americans will spend six and a half percent of all expenditures on "clothing, accessories, and jewelry." Is this reasonable?

6. Do I sometimes (or often) put myself in situations where I know it is likely that I will spend money on things I had not earlier known I "needed"? (For example, by reading mail catalogues, sales flyers, or by entering bookstores or clothing stores or stopping at the bakery or deli.)

7. *Luxury* comes from an older word which can mean lust or habitual indulgence. What does it mean to say that yesterday's luxuries are today's necessities?

8. Thomas Chalmers, preaching one of the great sermons of the century, talked about "the expulsive power of new affections." Mean while, Jesus tells of the man cleansed from one demon who ended up with seven when nothing filled his empty heart. It's important that new loves replace old ones. And truly abundant life comes with feeling God's own affections. Is my *affective life* (those things which I hold dear) changing in any way as I review my relationship to money?

9. Are some new categories in my budget replacing old ones? What does this mean?

10. It is natural to pray for things I need and do not have. How should I pray over things I have already received? (After all, we don't oil a wheel that isn't squeaking.)

11. John Schneider in *Godly Materialism* says that wealth isn't all that bad, and that God expects us to live like kings and queens of His creation. Yet in 1 Timothy 6:10 we are cautioned that the love of money is the root of all evil. How do I put this all together?

12. In the same book, John Schneider suggests that Jesus and his family were, for the time and place, basically middle-class. Did Jesus then freely impoverish himself to carry out his public ministry?

13. The purpose of pruning a tree or vine is to produce more and/or better fruit. How can this be applied to the pruning of a budget?

14. John Wesley, over a period of several years, saw his university income increase fourfold, yet he kept his expenditures constant and gave away the difference. What is my reaction to this?

15. One important thing God has shown me recently about truly abundant life in Jesus is _____.

End of cluster 2.2.
Go on to cluster 2.3.

Cluster 2.3

What Did Jesus Just Say?

Wesley K. Willmer, Vice President of University Advancement, Biola University, reviewed the number of times various topics were mentioned in the Bible. He found that believing or believers appeared 272 times, pray or prayer 371 times, love or loving 714 times, with possessions and giving appearing 2,172 times. He estimates that 17 of the 38 parables are about possessions.

Luke's gospel, which some consider especially directed to "better-off" believers, keeps the issue of money front and center.

So it's a little surprising that money is considered such an awkward topic in the church. Or maybe it's not so surprising after all. As Mark Twain observed, "Most people are bothered by those passages in Scripture which they cannot understand; but as for me, I always noted that the passages in Scripture which trouble me most are those which I do understand."

This cluster of questions considers a number of Jesus' pointed statements about money. As you reflect on these topics, don't forget that we're not alone on this journey. Jesus came not to make us feel bad, but to show us a better way. Because he loved us. It's God's love for us which gives us courage to talk about the real issues in our lives.

1. In the parable of the soils, Jesus refers to good spiritual growth being crowded out by "the deceitfulness of riches" (Matt. 13:22, KJV). What does this suggest to me?

2. In Matthew 6:24, Jesus personifies the power of wealth, calling it Mammon. In what ways is the power of money *god-like*?

3. Jesus said we will always have the poor with us. (You might compare Mark 14:3-11 and Deuteronomy 15:4-11.) What does this mean?

4. Jesus implies in Luke 18:24-25 that it is virtually impossible for a rich person to enter the Kingdom. How are we to understand this?

5. Jesus says to give Caesar what belongs to Caesar (Luke 20:20-26). Is there a relationship between money and civic duty?

6. When Jesus sends out the Twelve (Luke 9:1-6) and then the seventy-two (Luke 10:1-9) to preach and to heal, he instructs them to live off the hospitality of others. Is this in any way a model for us? Why or why not?

7. In Luke 16:9 Jesus tells us to use our money to make friends. Is friendship something that can be bought?

8. The story of Zacchaeus (Luke 19:1-10) appears to be Luke's (and Jesus') answer to the question of how a rich person can enter the Kingdom. What is the answer?

9. Jesus and the Twelve apparently had a common purse kept by Judas Iscariot (see John 12:4-6). Is this a model for us today? Why or why not?

10. What does Jesus probably mean when he says that where our treasure is, there our hearts will be as well (Matt. 6:21)?

11. If Joseph of Arimathea or Nicodemus had decided to endow Jesus' public ministry with a thousand talents of silver annually (worth perhaps $5 million dollars today), how do I suppose Jesus would have responded?

12. The parable of the Judgment (Matt. 25:31-46) would seem to imply that good works (how one actually spends time and money) impact salvation. Yet salvation comes through grace. What is my response to this?

13. Luke 4 presents the major temptations of Jesus by Satan. One of these was to wealth and power. This temptation, we must assume, was genuine—and we are told (Luke 4:13) that Satan leaves Jesus only for a time. So it is likely that again and again Jesus was faced with the powerful allure of money, much as we are. What were his strategies and resources for confronting this?

14. In Luke 21:1-4, why exactly does Jesus commend the widow who gave the two tiny copper coins (*lepta*, now a name for a subatomic particle)?

15. Jesus says (Luke 12:15) that life is not a matter of abundant possessions. The seventeenth-century poet and devotional writer Thomas Traherne says that since God is utterly generous, He would be most liberal with the very best gifts—hence the commonest things are in fact the most precious ones. How is the superabounding, joyous, authentic Christian life *not* a matter of money and what money can buy?

End of cluster 2.3.
Before going on to level 3, take time to reflect on the level 2 Gateway Question on the next page.

Level 2 Gateway Question

Before you go on to level 3, take some time to reflect on the following Gateway Question.

As was the case with the level 1 Gateway Question, if you feel comfortable with your answer to this level 2 Gateway Question, then go on to level 3 for the next round in your reflection experience.

However, if you feel some reservations in your answer to this question, you might want to go back through a few of the topics in level 2 that you could profitably spend more time on. Or you might find that some of the questions raise additional issues for you now. Take your time until you are comfortable. Then come back and review this question once again.

Gateway Question for level 2:

Do I have a significantly new understanding of Jesus' statement that one is more blessed (happy) in giving than in receiving? And am I witnessing changes in how I spend my money, changes which point toward a more trusting relationship with God?

CHAPTER 7

Level 3 Overview

Exploring Discipleship

You may have seen the popular bumper sticker: "He who dies with the most toys wins."

Then came the counter-sticker: "He who dies with the most toys is still dead."

Existential debate on the superhighways of life.

Sometimes as we zoom along life's journey, it's hard to sort out what's important and what's not. Then all of a sudden, in the most common places, we find ourselves encountering the true meaning of life in all its clarity.

A friend described a scene that took place as she stood in line at the store. Two little girls were at the cash register, each with a candy bar to buy. The clerk rang up the first girl's candy. There was a delay as coins were counted once, then twice. It became clear that the first little girl did not have enough money. The second little girl put her candy down on the counter and said, "Here, take this," and spilled her coins into the other girl's open hands. Receiving the money from her friend, the first girl dutifully handed it over to the clerk, who completed ringing up the sale and returned the change. The first girl smiled happily as she gave this change to her friend.

The second little girl handed her candy to the clerk, who rang up the sale. The clerk announced how much it would be. Once again, there was a delay as the coins were counted once, then twice. The surprise on the second little girl's face was followed by a tiny brave smile as the full impact of the situation hit her—now she didn't have enough for her own candy bar! The confused moment of silence that followed was interrupted by the clerk's announcement: "And I'm buying this one for you!"

Virtue, at its best, is contagious. The love that God shared with the world by sending his only Son began a movement that continues to spread throughout the globe. People become Christians because it's such good news that God really loves them.

These followers of Jesus Christ then set out on a journey. The goal is to know God better and to understand what it means to be transformed by the same power that raised Christ from the dead. Our transformation is part of the way that God is able to spread the good news. God chooses to work through the church to let others know how much they are loved.

But those of us who claim to be following Jesus Christ struggle during this process. And our struggles are public. George Bernard Shaw once issued this challenge:

> Why not give Christianity a trial? The question seems a hopeless one after 2000 years of resolute adherence to the old cry of "Not this man, but Barrabbas." . . . "This man" has not been a failure yet, for nobody has ever been sane enough to try his way.

Interestingly, Shaw does not suggest that a person must be crazy to follow Jesus faithfully. Just the opposite: he seems to imply that in order to follow Jesus a person must leave the craziness behind and become sane. When we see someone like the second little girl offering her friend all the money she had, and then the clerk paying for her candy—we remember that there is something so much more right than seeking our own good. Loving others can transform all those who are near us.

But in order to understand these ideas, we need to leave our brokenness behind and move toward a new kind of wholeness. There are statements in the Bible that indicate we are in a transition while on earth, being prepared to spend eternity in a completely different kind of environment. Beginning the process of transformation here, as a part of our relationship with Jesus Christ, makes us ready to be translated to the new reality that awaits us. And a theme in this transformation process is the idea that seeking the self's immediate good is not the way to find happiness; rather, losing one's life is the way to really find that life. This is a statement that might sound crazy to many people; yet it is really more sane than the conventional wisdom that preaches "me first." Truly, our minds must be renewed to understand the truth of all this.

In the first two levels of questions you have already worked through, you have been moving along a path of exploration. In this third level of topics, the path leads us into greater depth. Beyond the practical aspects of interacting with and around money, we move into the issues of trust, and responsibility, and opportunity. It is here, perhaps, that we can look for the kind of sanity that Shaw refers to, a clarity of values different than those proffered by a world gone mad with accumulation. Making these distinctions has never been easy. It has, however, always been the path to true abundance.

The first 15 questions in this third level might be summarized by the phrase, "Learning to Transfer Trust from Money to Christ in Serious Discipleship." Here, the issues raised challenge you to think through different aspects of where you have put your trust—and where you want to place your trust in the future.

In the second cluster, the topics look at an unpopular idea in our culture of immediate gratification. With a summary title of "The Cross of Gold and the Cross of Christ: Self-Denial and Discipleship," the goal is to consider where our own needs fit into God's scheme of things, especially when we compare them to the needs of others.

The third and last cluster of questions moves into the more upbeat idea that Jesus really did know what he was talking about. Here, we look at the joy that comes from faithfulness. Jesus did not come into the world to make us miserable. He tells us that his purpose was to give us real life, a life that is full (John 10:10). In following Jesus, we discover the freedom and the possibilities that come from knowing God better.

So, are you ready to continue? Then let's put it in gear and zoom ahead!

Cluster 3.1

Learning to Transfer Trust from Money to Christ

On one side of the Lincoln penny we read, "In God we Trust." On the other side we read, "E Pluribus Unum"—that is, "From the Many, One."

This last phrase, of course, acknowledges the hope for and the wonder of a true commonwealth emerging from the many different components of the early American republic.

As Christians, we may also understand the phrase as acknowledging the wonder of personal wholeness emerging from our personal brokenness as we follow Jesus Christ into abundant life.

Yet another possibility is to understand the words as acknowledging the wonder of the church: many are bound into one through the miraculous ongoing work of God the Holy Spirit.

Basic to this Christian discipleship is learning to trust God in all matters. In turn, that means trusting money less. Hopefully, you'll have some fun as you consider the following questions in this first cluster of level three, as you continue on this journey that leads you to find out more about you, and at the same time move toward more oneness with God through Jesus Christ!

1. Jesus says one must become like a child to enter the Kingdom (Matt. 18:3). How does this relate to my handling of money?

2. What is an annual income on which I would feel secure? How would I adjust if God asked me clearly to live on half that amount?

3. Is it possible to have too much life insurance? Why or why not?

4. We often pray, "Give us this day our daily bread." Does this mean we should not have pantries, home freezers, and potato cellars?

5. When in the recent past did God help me to find the extra money needed for a crisis? Is there a lesson for me in this experience?

6. If I was obliged to assign power of attorney granting another person the right to administer my finances, who would that person be and why?

7. Jesus tells us to ask largely that our joy may be full (see John 14:12-13 and 15:11). How would I explain this to a young child?

8. Personal wealth and endowment funds can be seed corn (which you do *not* want to eat) or they can be the talent one buries in the ground. How am I to understand the promise and the danger of wealth?

9. Jesus compared the Kingdom to a pearl for which one gladly trades in everything one has (Matt. 13:45-46). What are the *practical* implications of this?

10. When I'm visiting strange places, it is natural to check frequently on my wallet, money-belt, or purse. (Ah, still there, I may sigh.) What lesson do I find here?

11. Is it possible to be both prudent/practical/realistic and trusting/ risking/daring in the handling of money? Why or why not?

12. Alfred North Whitehead suggests that a natural sequence is to move from seeing God as the infinite void to seeing God as enemy, and then to seeing God as friend. But do I trust even friends with my money? Is anything more *mine* than my money? How does friendship relate to my money?

13. Identify several twentieth-century persons who have seemed free of the passion for money. What do they have in common?

14. A story popular several years ago tells of a mountain climber who slips, tumbles over the cliff's edge, and saves his life by grasping a shrub some feet down from the top, though hundreds of feet still stretch out beneath him. He hangs there for a moment, then shouts out for help. Soon a deep voice from above, out of sight, says to him, "This is God. I'll save you. All you have to do is let go and fall. Trust me." After a long spell the climber cries out, "Is there anybody else up there?" What is my response to this story?

15. How, in fact, am I finding it possible to trust God more and money less in my practical affairs?

End of cluster 3.1.
Go on to cluster 3.2.

Cluster 3.2

The Cross of Gold and the Cross of Christ

In *Bits and Pieces*, a publication of anecdotes and humor, a story described how an eight-year-old boy went to the pet store with his father. At last! He was going to have his own dog. The store manager took him over to a cage where five furry balls of energy bounced and played. The boy was delighted. As he stood looking at the fun, he noticed one little puppy curled up in the corner. "Why isn't he playing with the others?" the boy asked.

The manager shook his head. "That puppy was born with a bad leg. We're going to have to put him to sleep."

The boy looked frightened. "You're going to put him to sleep?"

The manager nodded.

The boy pulled his father to one side, and there was a whispered consultation. The two came back and the father announced, "We'll take the one in the corner."

"But why?" the manager asked. He turned to the boy and said, "That dog will never be able to run and play with a boy like you."

In answer, the boy pulled up his pant leg to reveal a brace and said, "Because I understand just what that puppy's going through."

Education can be expensive in more ways than one. A truism in teaching is that all real learning involves both gaining something and losing something. Otto Rank, the psychotherapist, has observed that there seems to be a spiritual law working in the universe. This law means that nothing can be really enjoyed unless something is given up or sacrificed for it.

Jesus said "If any man would come after me, let him deny himself and take up his cross and follow me. For whoever would save his life will lose it, and whoever loses his life for my sake will find it" (Matt. 16:24-25 RSV). It's a stretch to understand how that can be true. Perhaps the following points will be of help as you continue to learn about how you want to relate to both God and money.

1. There's a difference between "thorns in the flesh" and "crosses." The apostle Paul had no choice about his "thorn" (2 Cor. 12:7-8),

while Jesus voluntarily accepted the cross (Matt. 26:42). In our own lives, we have no control over the former, but we make a choice about the latter, freely accepting—or else refusing. What is my response to this?

2. Jesus says it is possible to gain the whole world and yet lose oneself (Luke 9:25). What would "world" and "self" mean here?

3. Jesus says that he came to provide abundant or full life (John 10:10b). What do we suppose such fullness involves, and how might it relate to self-denial?

4. A popular old gospel song refers to exchanging one's cross for a crown. Servanthood seems to precede reigning with Christ. What is my response to this idea?

5. Money, we recognize, has enormous power. Jesus came speaking and acting with what appeared to be measureless *spiritual* power. The New Testament resonates with the witness to the power also wielded by the obedient believer. Am I aware of spiritual power flowing through my own life? Through the lives of others close to me? In what ways do trust and self-denial play a part in the level of spiritual power I experience?

6. American philosopher Mortimer Adler, who converted to Christ very late in life, claims that the heart of Aristotle's ethics is the idea of *enough*. Adler of course believes Aristotle's wisdom to have wide relevance. Has God been training me in a new understanding of how much is enough? If so, how?

7. A cynical Frenchman observed that we find a little pleasure in the misfortune of even our best friends. The glory of the gospel is that we discover God's gracious self-sacrifice for us, and so become free to take genuine delight in all the good things that come to others. (It is not a zero-sum game, after all!) How am I learning to rejoice in good experienced by others?

8. The root word meaning of the word *sacrifice* is to make holy. True holiness of life, then, would seem to be inseparable from sacrifice. What are my associations, both positive and negative, with the idea of holiness?

9. In Matthew 11:28-30 Jesus speaks of his yoke as an easy one, and he promises that rest for the soul comes with wearing his yoke. How are yoke and cross related? Are they the same? Why or why not?

10. What major purchase have I decided against in order to free up money for compassionate giving?

11. In Luke 12:15 Jesus cautions against greed of all kinds. How would I define greed?

12. In the place of vicious appetites, which can never be satisfied, God offers in Christ those virtuous appetites which show themselves in a deepening and broadening love. New affections take root in us. What is my response to this concept?

13. The benevolence giving of a church, or giving to ministry which reaches beyond the immediate congregation, can be described as a measure of the selflessness of the church. Is my church unselfish? What leads me to my conclusion?

14. How is my life richer in the things that money cannot buy, richer than it was 12 or 18 months ago?

15. What has been the most radical insight into money which God has granted me out of Scripture or this study group?

End of cluster 3.2.
Go on to cluster 3.3.

Cluster 3.3

Joy through Compassion

There once was a really good salesman. He was so good that, as he interacted with God in prayer, he convinced God that he ought to be able to take a little of all he had with him when he died. God agreed, as long as whatever it was would fit in two suitcases.

The man thought long and hard, and then decided to sell much of what he had and fill the two suitcases with gold bullion. He packed them carefully in the cases, and sure enough not long after, he died.

He appeared at Heaven's gates and St. Peter told him that he would have to leave his suitcases at the door. "Just check with your boss," the salesman replied confidently.

St. Peter was gone a moment, and then returned. "Okay, you can bring them in. But you're going to have to show me what's in them before I let you through."

The man stepped forward and opened the cases. St. Peter's serious expression changed to one of puzzlement. His surprise showed on his face as he asked the salesman, "But why would you want to bring bricks?"

It's safe to say that this salesman's transformation was still in process as he left his earthly dwelling to travel on heavenly streets paved with gold. We are all involved in rethinking what *is* valuable and what only *seems* valuable.

We remind ourselves that Jesus said it is a happier thing to give than to receive. As we unlearn old habits—the so-called common sense of the world with its shortsighted values—and learn the new habits of Christian discipleship, the fruit of God's Spirit begins to show in our lives: love, joy, peace, kindness, self-control, patience, faithfulness, gentleness, goodness.

The perfect ends of God's work in us are not poverty, meanness, tightness, worry, bitterness, depression, and misery, but rather the very affections which characterize God's own nature. Chief among these are love, joy, and peace—love for God leading us to love our neighbors; joy as God's Spirit moves out from our depths in supernatural power; peace in the unquenchable assurance of God's goodwill, now and forever.

As you consider these points in this third cluster of level three, our hope is that you will find how much these fruits of the Spirit are growing and blossoming in you!

1. One cannot possibly attend to all human needs—can one? To echo an ancient question, "Who is my neighbor?"

2. Have I been able to retrench in significant ways as I have reworked budgets in the past year? As a result, have I found I could get along with less in order to help others more? How and why?

3. Was it right of the father to slaughter the fattened calf when the spendthrift son returned home? (See Luke 15:11-32.) Why or why not?

4. Was it appropriate for the vineyard owner to pay latecomers the same wage as he paid those who had worked all day? (See Matt. 20:1-16.) Why or why not?

5. Some authors have suggested a sliding scale for tithers. As income increases, second, third, and fourth tenths should be given annually on the increased portions of income. Does this make sense? What kind of sliding scale might work for me?

6. What is a good balance between *impulse* and *discipline* in matters of giving?

7. Should I consult with others before making major donations? If so, with whom, and why?

8. Jesus said that he was sent to the lost sheep of the house of Israel, yet went on to heal the Syro-Phoenician woman's daughter (Mark 7:24-30), and had good words to say about a certain Samaritan (Luke 10:25-37). In matters of compassion, what is my "Israel," and what is my "Syro-Phoenicia" or "Samaria?"

9. When and why do I most enjoy giving?

10. As my stewardship has become more central to my discipleship to Jesus Christ, how has my discipleship been impacted in other ways?

11. If I were asked to raise, personally, a thousand dollars for Christian mission, how would I proceed? How would I encourage other members of my church to do the same?

12. What do I now understand my wealth consists of? What has changed in me?

13. What portion of my income—and what portion of my wealth—is it proper and good for me to keep for myself, and how do I justify keeping this part?

14. How does one come to love God?

15. How does one come to love one's "neighbors"?

The Beginning

PART 3

An Overview of Small Groups

CHAPTER 8

A Very *Brief History of Small Groups*

The human quest for self-improvement is summed up well by a "prayer for the day" that *USA Weekend* reported hearing on WGMS radio in Rockville, Maryland: "Lord, make me the kind of person my dog thinks I am."

And people have employed small groups throughout history to move themselves from where they were to where they wanted to be.

In the beginning . . . In preparing a brief reflection for a weekly staff Bible study, we were struck with how important this theme of community, the ultimate goal of the small group structure, has been in the history of God's involvement with humans. On one very deep level, we've concluded that the saddest verse in the Bible is in Genesis. God has come into the garden "in the cool of the day" (Gen. 3:8, NIV). God calls to Adam and Eve, who are now hiding after having eaten from the apple. Understanding what has happened, God utters the anguished question that defines history from that point on: "What is this you have done?" (Gen. 3:13, NIV).

But by God's grace, the story does not end there. Moving forward to Revelation, we read of the new heaven and the new earth. Here the ultimate point of the ongoing story, including Jesus Christ's life, death, and resurrection, is summed up: "And I heard a loud voice from the throne saying, 'See the home of God is among mortals. He will dwell with them; they will be his peoples, and God himself will be with them' " (Rev. 21:3, NRSV). Community between God and people at long last is fully restored.

Of course, history records a lot of events between that tragedy in the garden and the restoration of community foretold in Revelation. And if you look for the role small groups have played during these centuries, it's surprising how often they surface.

Small groups in the Old Testament. A number of those who have specifically reviewed the role of small groups in the Bible note that Moses, on the advice of his father-in-law, divided the people of Israel into smaller units for administrative purposes (Exod. 18).

The social fabric was different during those days, and so people did not need to organize themselves into a Tuesday night discussion session in front of the fireplace in someone's comfortable living room. But missions professor Charles Mellis points out in his book *Committed Communities* (Mellis, 1976, pp. 9-10) that we hear about families as distinct units in the Old Testament. There was Noah's family, and there was Joshua's family, which was referred to in Joshua's famous line, "As for me and my household, we will serve the Lord" (Josh. 24:15, NRSV), and there were bands of a chosen few, such as Gideon's army and David's fighting men. There were even Samuel's group of prophets (1 Sam. 10:10 and 19:20) which continued at least through Elijah's time (2 Kings 2:3).

Small groups in the New Testament. Of course, experts point to the way Jesus organized his own ministry to emphasize the important role that small groups played at that time. There is a general consensus that when Jesus chose the 12 disciples, and within that group the three, those of us who would be his followers were being given a pattern for deeper growth.

The small groups that Jesus formed were not an alternative to his public ministry. Instead, they complimented Jesus' outreach to the general population. In *Community of the King,* scholar and professor Howard Snyder points out that Jesus kept his disciples with him, both when he was addressing huge crowds or talking with them in a private room, developing a "harmonius small group/large group rhythm."

Snyder says this pattern was then continued in the early church. In Acts 5:42 we learn that the first group of believers got together both in the temple and also in small group meetings in people's homes. The small-group design was spread to other areas, he notes, as indicated by the fact that Paul often refers to the "church that meets in your home" when he is writing to different sets of believers (Snyder, 1977, p. 147).

First century through A.D. 1000. The early believers were organized into small groups because this structure also furthered survival in a hostile culture. For the first 300 years after the founding of the church, Christians found themselves in societies in which it was not unusual for them to be persecuted for their beliefs. It wasn't until the declaration of the emperor Constantine in A.D. 313 that Christianity became the official religion, and being a Christian no longer required some level of immediate personal risk.

At that point, according to theologian and sociologist Julio de Santa Ana in *Good News to the Poor*, the church became divided into two realms. There was a Christianity practiced by the general population, and there were the more dedicated bands who gathered into monasteries (Santa Ana, 1997, p. 76).

Remarkable stories came out of these intentional groups who gathered to know God ever more deeply. Mellis recounts the effect of the Irish monks, a youth movement of those early centuries which has been credited with evangelizing Europe (Mellis, 1976, p. 23).

A.D. 1000 through 1800. By the thirteenth century, reform movements within the church were springing up in new orders of friars, such as the Franciscans and Dominicans.

In the fifteenth century, in addition to the German princes, small groups of laymen read copies of Martin Luther's 95 Theses, the document that served as a flash point for the Protestant Reformation. At the same time Francis Xavier and Ignatius Loyola were leading a Catholic Reformation from within the structure of the church.

Small groups were a vital part of the way reform leaders organized their followers. Some groups among the Anabaptists, such as the Amish, the Hutterites, and the Mennonites, emphasized withdrawal from the larger society. In such cases, the fellowship itself became a group distinct from its surroundings.

These early reform movements sometimes had an impact beyond their immediate participants. According to Mellis, John Wesley "partly patterned his famed small-group 'classes' on the *Banden* of the Moravians, which were voluntary fellowship communities within the larger total community" (Mellis, 1976, p. 43).

An interesting point surfaces about Wesley's initial impulse for founding these small group meetings. Historian Kenneth Scott Latourette wrote in his book, *A History of Christianity*, that the groups were "Originally mainly a device for raising money." Wesley scholar Howard Snyder told us in private correspondence that the penny a week which participants were expected to bring to the meetings first was used to pay off a debt on the Methodist preaching house in Bristol, and later was used to help poor people and support itinerant Methodist preachers.

Snyder notes that Wesley very quickly moved beyond this initial fund-raising idea and practical aim for the groups to an emphasis on the discipleship of the participants. Latourette's description of these classes indicates that they functioned in the Wesleyan discipline as "primarily a means of intimate fellowship for spiritual and moral growth under the direction of a mature Christian" (Latourette, 1953, pp. 1026-1027).

Even so, for our current purposes, it is fascinating to see that there is such a positive precedent in the history of the church for a small group movement that combined both faith and money.

Small groups in early America. The Wesley small groups were imported to America. They joined traditions that came with the Puritans and members of the pietistic movement as they escaped persecution in Europe. Baptist prayer meetings are one example of these activities.

Further, Robert Wuthnow points out in his study that American culture was impacted by the fact that immigration to America often happened in the form of small groups, either as a family unit or as a group of neighbors emigrating from their community in their former country to a community in their newly adopted one (Wuthnow, 1994b, pp. 41-42).

In the small towns that were typical of much of America until World War II, the church was often the social center of the community. Social and spiritual activities were organized into committees, men's and women's societies, and Sunday school classes. Even in urban areas, life for those new to this country was often organized around the church or parish, again because of the common ethnic heritage evident in the activities centered in the church.

Small groups in the United States, 1960s through the present. Earlier, we talked about the change that took place in American culture as people moved from extended families to the relatively isolated nuclear family. This change was spurred in large part by the affluence that spread through this country after World War II. Now people could afford to move farther from their place of work, and to travel to go to church or to shop.

In the 1960s and 1970s, Wuthnow says, an intentional small group effort began (Wuthnow, 1994b, pp. 43-44). Perhaps this type of organizing activity took place at that time as a reaction to what many already sensed was the growing change in the way American society was organized, a change that produced increasing isolation.

Today, estimates vary on how many people are involved in small groups. Wuthnow's study found that 40 percent of American adults are involved in some type of intentional small group. Further, of the 60 percent who indicated that they were not involved in a group, 39 percent said they had been involved in such a group at some time in their lives (Wuthnow, 1994b, pp. 45, 48).

Reflections. There are many ways to think about history. Those of us who claim the Christian faith see it in the context of a story that began in Genesis and moves toward Revelation. We are part of a plan that involves God's reaching out to human beings, and human beings becoming transformed into folks who can become friends with God through the power that raised Jesus Christ from the dead.

History is the combination of many individual stories and how they interact with each other. One key way individuals interact is by gathering together into smaller groupings to help them make sense of their roles in the big picture.

The next chapter is designed to help you anticipate some of the ways in which you can organize your own contribution to this stream of history by having the best small group possible as you consider the vital topic of faith and money.

CHAPTER 9

How to Run an Effective Small Group Discussion

We once read about a zookeeper who had to find out how a particular monkey kept escaping. The monkey lived on an island surrounded by a moat. The design looked good on paper, but the keeper routinely had to track the monkey down in some other part of the zoo because the monkey frequently got off the island. So the zookeeper kept a sharp eye out. One day he watched as the monkey came to the edge of the water and began waving a banana over his head. Not long afterward, a moose from another part of the compound entered the moat and swam over to the monkey. The clever monkey stuffed the banana in the moose's mouth, climbed on its back, and was carried to freedom!

Human beings also are creative in the pursuit of something they want to do. We say proudly that we can do just about anything we set our minds to. That phrase, "set our minds to," is a key element in whether we succeed, of course. As a friend of ours used to say, "People *do* what they want to do." If people want to go to the moon, for example, they organize themselves to do it. However, in the conversations with our friend, the focus was more on the fact that if people are not pursuing justice on a variety of levels, is it because they can't—or more simply, because they don't want to?

In our present discussion with you, we are talking about putting together a small group that helps those involved to explore their feelings and attitudes about God and money. We assume that you *do* want to succeed in this activity. So in the following pages we'll give you some tips we've gleaned both from experience and from the writings of others. You can use these ideas, perhaps in combination with your own accumulated information, to have your best small group yet!

In the next chapter we'll provide you with a step-by-step guide that describes how you can run a small group session using the topics provided in this book. But first, let's talk a little about how to get a small group ready to talk, and also about some of the challenges that might be involved.

Details for Success

The invitation. Robert Wuthnow's research on small groups found that 60 percent of the people participating in a small group joined because someone they knew asked them. That was true even if there were announcements from the pulpit and invitations printed in the church newsletter and bulletin. People were also influenced by whether they had "The desire to grow as a person" or were "Wanting to become more disciplined in your spiritual life." Still, a key factor was whether someone they knew had asked them to join (Wuthnow, 1994b, pp. 84-85).

So, to form your small group, it will be a good idea to talk to other people about it. Will the group be formed especially to discuss money and values? If so, will you ask people you know from your own church, or from some other circle in which you are active?

One congregation with which we worked, introduced into an ongoing class the system of considering one of the money and values discussion topics every other week, alternating with the regular Sunday school lesson. Another congregation chose to set aside a brief time at the start of each church council session. This approach might be particularly fruitful for administrative groups of the church, such as the council, the finance committee, or the trustees. These committees often have the responsibility to run the "business" of the church, and it is very easy for them to separate their tasks from the spiritual aspect of their responsibilities. Of course, your church may also have a small group structure in place that can make use of these topics.

Composition. If you decide to use the topics in a group that is already meeting, you don't have to worry about who might be asked to join the discussion. If an ongoing Sunday school class or a standing church administrative structure decides to use the topics, then the participants are already defined. If you are going to organize a group particularly to talk about the discussion questions offered in this book, then you have quite a bit of room in which to move.

Many church groups often involve people of the same gender and of similar age groups. There is something to be said for this approach, where circumstances are alike and people can benefit from hearing how other people are handling the situations they find themselves in. These gatherings are quite natural, and if you find it easy to put together a group in this way, full steam ahead!

However, some experts suggest that there are good reasons to try to get different types of people together. Jeffrey Arnold, a pastor and author of *The Big Book on Small Groups*, proposes that the very nature of Christian faith draws different people together. He writes, "The common bond that links Christians together is not the similarity of our past, but the convergence of our future." He goes on to say, "God's plan for community building in the church is that people who would not necessarily be friends in another setting come together and start the long, difficult process of becoming co-disciples" (Arnold, 1992, p. 75, 102).

Such a varied group can provide new insights to the participants. In one women's Bible study we had, there were both rich and poor members. When reading the New Testament, they came across a passage where Paul mentioned his experience in prison. The financially better-off ladies were surprised at the very concrete response the other ladies had. Instead of talking about the abstract need to suffer for our faith, the financially poorer ladies expressed personal concern for Paul, based on their own experiences of having relatives in prison. After more conversations, the group then started to write to these sons and nephews who were in jail, sending Bibles when they were requested.

Gareth Weldon Icenogle has strong feelings on whether people should mix in small groups. In his theological consideration of the area, he says that groups that do not provide for bringing people together across age and gender differences might wonder whether they have a clear understanding of who God is and God's purpose and mission. He also raises the concern of whether "the liberating Spirit of God" will be able to exercise "a full width and breadth of ministry" in groups where all types are people are not gathered together and free to explore the fullness of God (Icenogle, 1994, p. 109).

So, depending on your own circumstances, you might want to be open to involving people of different backgrounds, including age groups and both genders, as you organize your group. On the other hand, you may have a good reason to define a safe space in which some people who are quite similar in important ways can reflect together on this challenging area of faith and money.

In addition to thinking about which people should participate, you will want to decide how large your group should become. Jesus chose 12 disciples to be his main small group. John Wesley focused on that number as well. Wuthnow says that evidence indicates trust appears to be stronger in groups that are smaller than it is in larger groups. He suggests that this supports the idea that "heart-to-heart sharing becomes much more difficult when a group becomes larger than fifteen or twenty people" (Wuthnow, 1994b, p. 154).

The people involved will also help define the size of group you will want to think about. You may want to limit your group to six couples, for a total of 12 people, but find that a group with ten single and married people combined is as high as you want to go. If the group is just starting out, then a smaller grouping will probably have an easier time establishing trust among the members.

How large should a group grow before it divides? On the other hand, how long should the group be open to new members before it closes off that option? Again, you will be the best judge. In fact, given the nature of a discussion on money and values, you may want the group's membership to remain stable during the course of the discussion. Meanwhile, you may also have a clear expectation that those in the group are being prepared to serve others by leading additional groups. In the guide that follows in the next chapter, there is a suggestion that if several groups are using these topics in a coordinated fashion, then the leaders of each group should form a training and support group for each other. The leaders can then work with their individual groups as well. You can decide if such a model works for you.

The setting. Deciding where you want to have the group deserves careful attention. If your church is conveniently located for all the group participants and has a comfortable, informal room that affords the necessary level of privacy, then you might want to reserve this space on a regular basis.

You might also want to have the meetings in someone's home. Here, people can also gather in comfort, forming a circle with each person being able to see the faces of all the others present.

Whatever place you choose, the groups will benefit by being removed from distractions such as televisions or stereos, ringing telephones, or the traffic patterns of other members of the household or other people who are in the church building. Consider arrangements for such necessities as child care and convenient rest rooms, and avoid scheduling conflicting responsibilities such as having to leave "for only a few minutes" to pick up a child from a regular activity. Referring to these kinds of distractions, Icenogle says, "Some of these interruptions may not be preventable, but many are" (Icenogle, 1994, p. 25).

The group contract. Whether you know it or not, your group will work out a "contract" or "covenant" about how the group is going to be run. The experts say your chances of having a successful group will increase dramatically if you make a point to work out these details rather than just let them develop. As Wuthnow writes, "Formal structures create a space, as it were, for people to get to know each other. Trust can develop more easily because people do not have to worry much about group goals" (Wuthnow, 1994b, p. 159).

Concepts for Success

Purpose. One key decision, for example, is to be sure everybody shares the same purpose for the group. Dan Williams, who both supervises and trains small group leaders, notes that it's important to clarify the purpose early for several reasons. For example, by identifying expectations, those who do not feel comfortable with the focus are able to leave, while others may be attracted to that particular goal (Williams, 1991, p. 114).

A clearly stated purpose can set the tone for constructive group interaction. In their academic textbook, university professors Steven A. Beebe and John T. Masterson note, "Without an overarching group goal, individual agendas are likely to be more important than the group agenda. The goal should be one that excites the group and fosters a team approach rather than an individual approach" (Beebe and Masterson, 1997, p. 19).

Having mixed motivations among group members is not necessarily a problem—unless it prevents some of the members of the group from pursuing the stated purpose. It's easy to imagine what could happen in a situation where some participants are concerned primarily about spiritual growth while others are looking for social networking. Several people have come to talk in depth about a particular passage from the Bible, but a few others keep wanting to talk about good baby-sitters and places to get the best deal on disposable diapers. There are going to be some frustrated people, no matter how the discussion goes!

So it is good to be clear why people are coming together. In the guide that follows, it suggests that you have everyone agree that the first portion of the evening will be spent on the scheduled topic, with the goal being to move toward authentic sharing among the group participants. Then the members can talk with each in a more general way after the time set aside for this meeting's discussion topic is over.

Clyde Reid suggests there are six key points that any group should agree on in order to develop a workable group contract: (1) purpose; (2) size and composition; (3) time factor; (4) level of interaction; (5) leadership (although he points out that does not necessarily mean "a leader"); and, (6) group disciplines (Reid, 1969, p. 34-41).

By group disciplines, he means things like whether or not people will be upset if everyone is not there until a half hour after the scheduled starting time, and whether refreshments are served during the discussion or after it.

Arnold also talks about what he calls "ground rules." He suggests that the group clearly state such ideas as, "We should try to be as honest as possible with each other within this group" and "We will never talk about others behind their backs" (Arnold, 1992, p. 188).

Having a group contract also may give participants permission to share at deeper levels than they otherwise would. Since money is a difficult topic for most of us, it may be harder for the group to move beyond superficial levels of sharing without a conscious effort. If there is a clear discussion that leads to agreement among the group members that people are free to share their feelings, that it is not fair to criticize or laugh at what another person says (unless that person is laughing first), and that the goal is to understand rather than judge, then a high level of trust can be established fairly early on in the group's life.

Leadership. Experts agree that leadership will emerge in a group whether a formal decision is made or not. The personalities in the small group will define what type of leadership is effective. Once again, your group will be unique. There may be an individual who has a gift for drawing out the best in everyone present. As a result, all the members of the group feel most comfortable with this person's style and prefer to have this one individual lead the group. You might also have a small team who can cover for each other. Or your group might be such that the relationships are well established and the leadership can be shared among all those present.

Nathan W. Turner, who has pastored and now practices psychology, offers a helpful idea. In his book, *Leading Small Groups: Basic Skills for Church and Community Organizations*, he suggests the leadership dynamic moves from individual responsibility to group responsibility. The spectrum moves from "Leader decides—announces decision to group" all the way to "Group defines limits—group decides" (Turner, 1996, p. 31). Your group may move along this spectrum during the course of its existence.

A handbook from Augsburg-Fortress Press provides a step-by-step training manual for small group leaders. One interesting point is that David Mayer and his coauthors opt to use the term "facilitator" rather than leader. The writers suggest that the term is more descriptive, less threatening, and does not imply the usual level of control associated with the term "leader," even though they acknowledge, "At times a facilitator needs to lead" (Mayer, 1995, p. 50).

The individual style of the leader does not change the fact that there is a definite role for *leadership*. As Icenogle notes, "Purposeless groups fail. Leaderless groups also fail. Small groups need direction, purpose and leadership. There can be multiple leaders in a small group, but there cannot be a healthy group without leadership. Leadership gives direction and meaning" (Icenogle, 1994, p. 45).

Reid suggests several important parts of leadership. One is that the leadership should affirm the value of the group's participants. Another is the role of setting bounds on behavior. And a third is to help the group reflect and move on when it seems to be stuck (Reid, 1969, pp. 85-87).

It takes confidence to put yourself at risk in the presence of another person, let alone a whole group of people. Your small group will be successful if people involved in it feel free to share their feelings. One way to insure that kind of atmosphere is to affirm and encourage the participants. If there is a single leader, each participant will need to feel respected and affirmed by this individual. If the leadership is more widespread, a shared ethic that the group as a whole is worthwhile, and that each participant is valuable, is very important.

As Bill Donahue of the Willow Creek Church Small Groups Team points out, "It is important to create an atmosphere where group members affirm and encourage one another, build each other up in Christ, and help each other grow" (Donahue, 1996, p. 88).

On the next few pages, we are going to be talking about some negative behaviors that can short-circuit your group's interactions. One of the roles of leadership is to provide guidance when these behaviors show up. There are certain boundaries that should be established as your group members talk with each other. The leadership of the group has the responsibility to let participants know if they feel those boundaries may have been crossed. For example, if someone abruptly changes the topic away from meaningful group interaction, and there is not general support for that new direction of conversation, or if someone is abusive to another person, the leadership needs to provide guidance with regard to the inappropriate behavior.

Finally, sometimes groups get stuck. They seem to be going along fine, and then they aren't. At that point, it's the responsibility of the leadership to ask as basic a question as one suggested by Reid: "We seem to be having difficulty; what do you think is really going on here?" (Reid, 1969, p. 87.)

Icenogle refers to the work of small group specialist Dan Williams who provides the helpful idea that each member of the group will have a positive contribution to make to the effective working of the group (Icenogle, 1994, p. 86).

Even if one person begins as the leader, it may be that the group can grow to the point where leadership can be shared among all present. In fact, according to the academic study by Gerard Egan, "the function of the leader in the contract group is to become less and less a leader and more and more a member" (Egan, 1970, p. 135). That idea is particularly true in a group where you are gathered to talk about the problems and challenges of integrating your attitudes toward money with your relationship to God. All the group participants should remember that the leader will have as much need to be able to share openly and receive feedback from others as does every other member of the group.

Rather than get too overwhelmed with the responsibilities of leadership, we can be comforted by one of the conclusions drawn by Wuthnow as a result of his study: "It does not take a great deal of special knowledge or skill to make a small group function well. . . . the important finding is that caring and informal friendships are the key to an effective group, not following some elaborate management plan" (Wuthnow, 1994b, p. 344).

Preparation for Success

Behaviors in small groups. We're all Christians. We all want to grow spiritually. We all want to come to terms with our attitudes toward God and money. Therefore, we should all get along just fine. Right? Not likely!

We are all growing, it is true. But we are all at different places. C. S. Lewis made an interesting point in *Mere Christianity*. He said that some people will look at Person A who is not a Christian but who is a really attractive individual, and then look at Person B who is a Christian but is a real pain. The wrong conclusion that can be drawn from this comparison is that Christ does *not* make a difference in a person's life. Not so, says Lewis. Rather, each person should be compared with himself or herself. In the case of Person A, think of how much more she could become by coming into relationship with Christ! And in terms of Person B, why think how much worse he would be if he did not know Christ! As with individuals, so it is with small groups made up of those individuals. Icenogle points out that every group has a "bright and dark" side. The goal is to make a point of leaving room for God's Spirit to work (Icenogle, 1994, p. 252).

Being prepared for some of the "dark" side behavior which people may bring to the group should provide a greater chance that all the participants can be affirmed. Let's look first at some of the negative behaviors that may crop up. And then we'll look at strategies to deal with them.

Fears. Reid concluded, as a result of his experience with small groups, that people can be afraid of being honest: "They fear that if they are really honest they may hurt someone, or the group may reject them. They fail to realize that honesty is the avenue to deep fellowship and acceptance as well" (Reid, 1969, p. 57).

People may mistakenly assume that a church group ought to have no evidence of conflict, or that happy groups are peaceful groups. Therefore, they may want to avoid conflict at all costs. Academics Beebe and Masterson point out, "It is a mistake to view positive group climate or group cohesiveness as a condition in which everyone is nice all the time. Quite the contrary. In a highly cohesive group, members know that they will not be rejected for their views and are therefore more willing to express them—even though expressing them may provoke disagreement" (Beebe and Masterson, 1997, 126).

As Jeffrey Arnold explains in *Starting Small Groups: Building Communities That Matter*, "Relationships need to be rooted deeply in God's bountiful mercy and grace. You cannot go deep when everybody is trying to create and live in a world that is more fantasy than reality" (Arnold, 1997, p. 98).

Others also emphasize this deep-seated feeling that prevents people from opening up. Therefore, it is important for all the participants in the group to be able to talk about their fears and to feel that the group has set up a safe zone for them to talk in an honest fashion.

Domination. Another behavior that may have to be dealt with is the tendency for one person to dominate the conversation. Talking a great deal can actually be a way for a person to avoid sharing his or her feelings at a deep level. An individual can control the direction of the conversation by insisting on taking up most of the time. Or a person can resist constructive change by absorbing the attention of all the group members, thereby avoiding feedback from them. This type of dominant behavior isolates the individual doing the excessive talking from the rest of the group. And people who are not allowed to participate in sharing themselves with the other members of the group may become angry or bored without communicating it, and eventually just fade away.

Role playing. Reid describes another problem: people who insist on taking on certain roles in the group. He describes the "group mother," the "group father," and the "group sweetheart." The person taking on one of these roles may not do all the talking in the group, but will limit the way people interact with him or her, and sometimes manipulate how people interact with each other. This type of person can demand attention in such a way that other members of the group are competing with each other for this person's attention. When this is going on, these members are not seeking to form healthy relationships with all the other members of the group (Reid, 1969, p. 104).

Superficiality. Some people may refuse to share very meaningfully. People should share only as much of themselves as they want with other members of the group. But a participant who feels ill at ease sharing with other people, particularly about their attitudes toward money, might use small critical comments or nasty laughter to keep the entire conversation on a superficial level. If the goal is to provide a safe zone for everyone present to share their deeper feelings, someone who will not allow others to talk at a deeper level can find a number of creative ways to prevent such sharing from occurring.

Anger. We all have different ways of reacting when we are threatened. Some of us withdraw. Others have outbursts. Generally, neither is a constructive response. The one that can be the most disruptive in a group, however, is the emotional outburst. We are not talking about an occasional expression of anger, either about an idea or even toward another person, if there is a commitment to work through the disagreement and move toward reconciliation. Here the group has a positive support role to play. Rather, we are talking about the individual who uses anger, or the threat of anger, to prevent uncomfortable topics from being raised. Soon it becomes easier for the group to avoid certain issues rather than risk this individual's display of temper, even if it means other members of the group cannot work through important issues in their own lives.

Strategies for Success

Any of these behaviors, as well as others, might surface in a small group that has gathered to grow deeper in their spirituality. It is particularly likely when we are exploring the not-often-discussed and emotionally confusing topic of money.

A small group does not have to be passive in the face of these types of behaviors. All the participants in the group should acknowledge up front that "God is not finished with me yet," as the saying goes. Any one of us can be in the offender's seat, depending on the situation. Understanding that we are all forgiven sinners, we should then take the advice offered in Galatians 6:1, as presented in the Amplified Bible:

> Brethren, if any person is overtaken in misconduct *or* sin of any sort, you who are spiritual [who are responsive to and controlled by the Spirit] should set him right *and* restore *and* reinstate him, without any sense of superiority *and* with all gentleness, keeping an attentive eye on yourself, lest you should be tempted also.

The strong goal is to bring the person into a restored relationship. In order to do that, you will need to talk to him or her.

Talk directly about problem behavior. Although we have talked about a variety of problem behaviors, it does not mean that one of them will surface in your particular group. However, once in a while, a leader, or those in leadership, may feel the need to take some initiative with a particular group member. This is true even if the problem is not a personal one between the leader and another group participant. In some of the behaviors we described above, it may be appropriate for the leader to talk with an individual about a particular behavior and the effect it has on the group. The individual may not be aware that the way he or she is acting is having a negative impact. In this case, the person should find the feedback helpful. If the individual does not want to change, however, there may be a role for a group discussion on the topic.

The leadership may also feel there is a problem that is beyond the scope of the group's ability. These small groups are not therapy groups. Part of the leader's task in setting boundaries is to help those in the group recognize what can and cannot be handled by all the group members. In some cases, a group member might be encouraged to seek assistance of a type which the group is not in a position to offer. The group's goal is to call the best out of each participant, and help people choose a direction that moves a problem toward solution. As Icenogle observes, the purpose of the group is to give hopefulness. A person who brings an ongoing problem should be guided into prayer, and then be encouraged to find healing through Christ. Accountability will keep the group hopeful. He writes, "Every group has its limit to how much pain it can bear in the name of Christ. The group must have touch with an abundance of hope in order to deal with limited pain. If the pain overcomes the hope, the group has taken on too much or they have forgotten their source of healing is in Christ and not in them" (Icenogle, 1994, pp. 351-352).

The sooner such conversations take place, the better, of course. A behavior that is only slightly irritating in its early stages can become a major source of trouble. If it is allowed to continue, other members in the group may work themselves up into a high level of frustration and unresolved anger about it.

How to confront someone. Turner suggests that conflicts are inevitable in groups. If there are no tensions in your group, there may be little trust among the group's participants. Instead of being afraid of conflict, Turner suggests that the leader recognize that there is energy involved, and use that energy in a productive manner. Among other strategies, he suggests that it's important to define how each person sees the situation, and how each feels about it (Turner, 1996, pp. 16, 106).

Reid provides a very useful description of how one might talk with someone whose behavior is a problem for you. He says that you should tell the person "openly how you feel about his behavior, how it affects you. You are not judging him; you do not need to know why he behaves the way he does. You simply share honestly with him how his behavior affects *you*" (Reid, 1969, p. 96).

The goal is restoration and increased understanding. There is not a place for vengeance by proving the other person wrong. When we go to the person, what do we say? Tell the person how the action in question is making us feel. We ought to be drawing the best out of each other at all times. If something we do is hurting another, we need to listen to the other person, and consider that person's needs as well as our own. And in such a conversation, the person who is acting in what is perceived as a hurtful way is offered a clear opportunity to work at restoring a positive relationship.

The more academic approach taken by Egan draws a similar conclusion from a study by another professional: "A study by Torrance suggests that confrontation will be more effective if it is positive and constructive rather than negative or merely evaluative" (Egan, 1970, p. 321).

Confidentiality. Part of the group contract should be the level of confidentiality that will be observed among the participants. Participants may assume that what is shared in the group will not be the basis for conversations elsewhere. However, you may want to make that understanding clear, to a greater or lesser degree.

This area of confidentiality includes conversations that two group members might have about a third. In our work, we use what we call the "Matthew 18 Principle." In that chapter, in verses 15-17, Jesus says that if someone offends you, you should go to that person. If the person listens, you have restored the relationship.

Within our organization we developed a policy based on this passage some time ago. Before that, we did not have a shared understanding among those on our staff about how we should relate to each other. We saw that when two people complained to each other about a third, but did not talk to the third person about the problem, it was destructive not only of personal relationships but also of working relationships. Now, when people are hired, we make it very clear that if a person has a problem with a coworker, that person should talk directly to that co-worker as a first step. If necessary, the person can then talk to a supervisor. Having these ground rules clear from the beginning has produced an improved work atmosphere.

This biblical principle has relevance for a small group as well. If a particular individual is having trouble with another individual in the group, the two people should take an opportunity to talk about it directly. One of those involved should take the initiative, perhaps during refreshments, to talk about any difficulty. Or the group as a whole, perhaps during a "business meeting" that is distinct from one of the regular gatherings, might set aside time to encourage the two people to explore their feelings.

In any case, the important goal is to encourage direct communication rather than create an atmosphere that encourages third-party gossip to swirl around the fringes of the group.

Put on love which binds in unity (Col. 3:14). Elizabeth O'Connor, as one of the founding members, has written about the experiences of the Church of the Saviour in Washington, D.C. Members of that church intentionally moved toward community with each other. In her book *Journey Inward, Journey Outward,* she reflects on the lessons they have learned which might be of help to others seeking to become more faithful to Jesus Christ.

She states that as Christians, we have a special challenge because:

We do not do the calling. Christ does the calling, and this is very threatening if we belong to his Church, because the people he calls are the people with whom we are to have intimate belonging. This gives us a strange assortment of people to be with. They are often not our idea of the ones God should be using to proclaim his Kingdom (O'Connor, 1968, pp. 24-25).

Even so, she says, because we have this common calling, we are in a position to take risks with each other. A key risk is to be honest with each other because we share the same faith. She goes on to point out that the people with whom we may have the most difficulty could be a problem because "they may be precisely the ones who have the most to tell us about ourselves. Modern psychology teaches that what we object to in others is often what can be found in ourselves." However, we have no choice, she advises, other than to work through these differences with each other, unless we are willing to pay the consequence: "When this happens, we forego being a people on a pilgrimage together" (O'Connor, 1968, pp. 25-26).

So, choosing to confront negative behavior is not an option for the Christian. We owe it to the other to call each other to grow more fully, and we owe it to ourselves to understand what the issues really are.

Providing space. Another useful approach to provide a positive setting for group members to be confident enough to share themselves is to set aside time for each person to talk. You might take a simple and direct approach to this need. For example, you might use the "poker chip" idea: everyone is given a number of chips, each worth a set number of minutes, which a person can "spend" in the evening's conversation at their own pace. One person times each group member's talking according to the chips thrown into the center of the group.

Another idea is to begin the evening with a set amount of time for each participant to share, and then open the discussion to general interaction after everyone has had a chance in this way.

In both cases, a simple kitchen timer can provide an objective measure of the time available for each person to talk.

Happily, Icenogle assures us that various disciplines are more necessary in groups that are still in the early stages of growing together. After awhile, the explicit structure becomes unnecessary because the group understands the value of disciplines within the group and internalizes these patterns of behavior. On this particular issue, he also strongly affirms the need to provide time for each individual to share. He sees having time for each person to talk not merely as a courtesy, but also a matter of justice (Icenogle, 1994, pp. 60-61).

Ready To Go

Our goal in providing you with the information in this chapter is to give you enough confidence to develop a good experience in your own small group. We haven't avoided the difficult topics, because we feel it is important that you not be surprised by them.

But don't let anything we've shared with you on the last few pages dampen your enthusiasm for the journey before you. As motivational author E. Joseph Cossman said, "Obstacles are things a person sees when he takes his eyes off his goal."

You stand on the threshold of an exciting voyage of discovery. Like any smart traveler, you've packed your umbrella and raincoat as well as your bathing suit and sunglasses. You can now set off, trusting that you're ready for whatever comes.

The next chapter provides you with some detailed information that is designed to make your small group a success!

CHAPTER 10

A Step-by-Step Guide for Organizing a Small Group to Use This Book

The following guide was developed as part of our work with congregations. That's the reason the outline below is so specific. We have adapted this outline for your use as part of *At Ease: Discussing Money and Values in Small Groups.*

This guide provides you with a detailed procedure for organizing a small group. It incorporates a lot of the information that we've shared with you in previous chapters. Of course, you may have extensive small group experience yourself. When you read these guidelines, then, you can compare our outline with what you have found works for you.

We've consulted other experienced people and presented our recommendations for the successful operation of a small group on faith and money. We suggest you think through the information included below. Feel free to organize your group in a way that works best for you.

We'd like to draw your attention to one part of the structure that hasn't been considered in the discussions on previous pages. We suggest that after the topic of the evening has been considered for the allotted time, you provide a time for people to share their personal joys and concerns, and then have a time for the group to pray together. This part of the evening can be very valuable for participants. We strongly recommend that you include such a prayer time in your agenda, even in your group that is focusing on the area of faith and money.

Once you've gone through the outline below, and you've formed your small group, you're ready to set out on your journey to work on your relationship with God and money. We're excited about all the possibilities in store for you.

The Small Group Guide

The simple format of the small group is designed to promote personal sharing. An important goal of the group is to encourage a safe atmosphere in which people are free to be honest about their struggles and to explore their thinking. People will not be required to share any financial information they do not want to.

The Role of the Small Group Leader

Each small group has a leader, or a team of leaders if that suits the particular situation better. It is important that this person is someone who has the respect of the other members of the group. This person leads the group participants through the meeting's schedule. The schedule has been kept intentionally simple. Even so, without this structure, the group can become merely a social exchange which will prove frustrating to those who are searching for active support in the area of attitudes toward money and possessions.

It is also important that the leader be a sensitive person who can draw in all participants. No one should be forced to talk until he or she feels comfortable in doing so. However, there are others who might feel too comfortable, monopolizing the conversation, and others who would talk if specifically invited to do so. The leader's goal is to strive for a balance that includes an opportunity for as many to talk as would like to.

The easiest procedure is for each person in the group to have an opportunity to respond to the topic of the week, possibly for a defined number of minutes. The rest of the discussion time can then be open. Even during open discussion, however, the leader's goal is to be sensitive to include all who might want to participate, and to guide those who might tend to dominate into sharing the floor with others.

Meeting Schedule

1. Each meeting begins with a reading of the litany (included at the beginning of this book).
2. After this reading, the leader states the topic for the week and invites each person to respond.
3. After everyone has had an opportunity to respond, the leader encourages general discussion on the topic.
4. About one hour after the beginning of the meeting, the leader opens the floor to joys and concerns of the group members, including prayer requests.
5. After this time of sharing, a time of general prayer follows.
6. When the prayer time is over, the topic for the following week is selected and is announced to the group (see topics in chapters 5 through 7).
7. The group adjourns until the next meeting, or for refreshments if they are being served.

Time and Length

The small groups are designed to meet weekly. However, the schedule of the group can be revised to meet the group's individual needs. A good plan is to have the entire discussion period be no longer than one to two hours, including prayer time and the selection of the next week's topic, unless the group mutually agrees to a different time frame. It is vital to take the schedules of the participants into account when setting up the meeting times

Location

An informal setting that will facilitate conversation, either in a home or another suitable location, is best to encourage sharing among the group members. Giving thought to a place that is conveniently located for all participants will improve the chances of regular participation by everyone.

Refreshments

Offering refreshments is optional. If refreshments are included, two stipulations are very important.

1. Refreshments are offered *after* the meeting, so that those with time limitations (small children or work-related responsibilities) can participate in the discussion and leave, as necessary, during refreshments.
2. "Simplicity" is the goal. Too often, participants in small groups feel obligated to "outdo" each other, placing a burden on the hosts and taking attention away from the original purpose of the group. If group participants make an agreement about what is an appropriate level of hassle-free refreshments, and then stick to it from meeting to meeting, no one is put on the spot.

The Size of the Group

An item of the group contract which members should consider early on is agreement on a workable size for the group. The initial group may want to see itself as providing experience for future small group leaders. As interest increases in this area of discussing faith and money, members of the original group could serve other interested people as leaders. The original group members might then want to continue meeting in a leaders' support group (see below).

Topics

One topic is selected and announced at the end of each week's meeting for the next week's meeting. This procedure allows people to think about the topic during the week if they like. Three possible ways to select the next week's topic are: (1) the group can work through the discussion topics as presented in chapters 5 through 7; (2) the group as a whole can choose among the available topics in a cluster; or (3) one member can select a topic by choosing a folded piece of paper with a number written on it. The topic that coincides with the number on the selected paper is then announced to the group.

There are three levels of questions, with three clusters of 15 questions in each level, for a total of 45 questions at each level, and a total of 135 questions altogether. When all topics in one cluster have been selected, the group can move to the next cluster within that level.

Since the group has been formed to talk about the area of faith and money, it's not a good idea to introduce topics other than those offered in chapters 5 through 7 as long as that remains the focus of the small group. The concern is that money is a difficult topic to discuss. If the group allows members to suggest alternative discussion ideas, the group's focus may wander. Those seriously wanting to explore the area of attitudes toward money and faith might end up unfairly frustrated.

After the group has gone through the questions in the three clusters at a particular level, the last question for each level is a Gateway Question. Taking the time to discuss this question allows the group as a whole to see if the members feel good about moving from the present level of questions to the next.

Evaluation

To help determine the future of the group, there are also evaluation questions. After the group has met for some time, perhaps after completing the first cluster or level, the group will benefit from considering such a question. The evaluation questions are different from the Gateway Questions. Whereas the Gateway Questions ask the group members to consider whether they want to move from one level to the next, the evaluation questions ask group participants to consider the role the group has played in their journey during this time period.

The suggested quarterly or semiannual evaluation question is: "What progress have I made in my attitudes toward God and money in the past ____ months? What role has the small group played in any changes which have occurred?"

At the last meeting of the year, an evaluation topic can also be discussed. That annual topic is: "Is the group profitable enough that we want to continue for the coming year?"

If a group were to move systematically through the three levels of questions, taking time for evaluation and the Gateway Question, each level of three clusters could take one year. The whole process could take three years. The group may want to design a shorter term by selecting only some questions in each cluster.

"Business Meeting"

Any group will have business details to take care of. Such concerns as child care or the meeting places for the next several months need to be worked out. After the evaluation session, the group can set aside time to make sure the details that strengthen the group's interactions are being tended to.

Social Gatherings

Once a quarter, the group might want to schedule a purely social time together. The activity can be defined by the desires of the group. The group might consider combining this social event with any other groups they are aware of, perhaps in the congregation, which are also considering the topics in *At Ease: Discussing Money and Values in Small Groups*.

Leaders' Meeting

If more than one small group in the congregation or some other structure is considering the topics in this book, then the leaders of all the groups may find it helpful to plan to meet regularly. The small groups might meet three weeks out of every month, with the small group leaders meeting on the fourth night of the month. Or the small group leaders might meet once a quarter. The purpose of the small group leaders' meeting is to share insights, to encourage one another, and to explore how each leader is responding to dynamics in each group. The small group leaders are in a unique position to help each other.

Checklist

A checklist for establishing a small group to discuss topics in *At Ease: Discussing Money and Values in Small Groups*.

____ 1. Recruit members who want to discuss the topics in chapters 5 through 7, up to a number that keeps the group a workable size.

____ 2. Decide on a regular, perhaps weekly, time frame and a convenient location, both that are mutually agreeable to the participants.

____ 3. In a congregation with more than one small group using *At Ease: Discussing Money and Values in Small Groups*, decide if there will be a leaders' meeting. If so, decide whether it will be the fourth week of each month or once a quarter, and whether it will be in addition to the regular small group meetings or instead of one meeting.

____ 4. Decide on who will provide leadership within the small group.

____ 5. Decide what, if any, commitments are expected with regard to regular attendance.

____ 6. Plan for child care if necessary.

____ 7. Schedule the date of both the next evaluation discussion and "business meeting," to attend to details related to the group meetings.

____ 8. Schedule the date of the small group's social event at the start of each quarter. Decide if this will be in addition to the small group meeting or instead of the small group meeting that week.

____ 9. Decide if there will be refreshments at each meeting. Seek a commitment on the part of anyone supplying refreshments that t hese will be kept simple, in order not to distract from the purpose of the small group.

SELECTED ANNOTATED BIBLIOGRAPHY
AND RESOURCE LIST

The following list includes a selected list of books that have either been
used in writing *At Ease: Discussing Money and Values in Small Groups*
or that we think may be of help to someone who wants to continue to
explore the area of faith and money. In addition, we include the names
of resources that might help you with more practical aspects of handling
money.

Arnold, Jeffrey. *The Big Book on Small Groups*. Downers Grove, Ill.:
InterVarsity Press, 1992. Jeffrey Arnold describes the different purposes
of small groups and how to train effective leaders.

―――――. *Starting Small Groups: Building Communities That Matter*.
Nashville: Abingdon Press, 1997. In this volume, Jeffrey Arnold provides a step-by-step plan for developing small groups. Each chapter
answers a question, from "What Are Our Goals?" to "How Will We
Market and Recruit?"

Beebe, Steven A. and John T. Masterson. *Communication in Small
Groups: Principles and Practices*. New York: Longman, 1997. This
academic textbook is in its fifth edition. It provides an overview of
small group communication, communication theory, and small group
operation.

Blue, Ronald. Ron Blue's work includes the book *Mastering Your
Money* (Nashville: Thomas Nelson, 1991) which focuses on the responsible handling of resources. His company, based in Atlanta, Georgia,

also provides financial planning services with a special emphasis on the role of giving.

Bolton, Robert. *People Skills: How to Assert Yourself, Listen to Others and Resolve Conflicts.* New York: Simon and Schuster, 1979. Robert Bolton discusses skills that are useful not only in leading small groups, but also in other life activities. The four sections of the book include: (1) basic communication skills; (2) listening skills; (3) assertion skills; and (4) conflict management skills.

Burkett, Larry. Larry Burkett is the author of numerous books on Christian financial management, including *Managing Your Money* (Chicago: Moody Press, 1991). He has a nationally syndicated radio show and founded Christian Financial Concepts (based in Gainesville, Georgia). His organization coordinates a nationwide network of trained, volunteer counselors who assist individuals in ordering their basic personal finances with an eye toward getting out of debt.

Dayton, Howard L. Jr. Howard Dayton has written *Your Money: Frustration or Freedom?* (Wheaton, Ill.: Tyndale House, 1971). In addition, he is the founder of Crown Ministries (Longwood, Florida), which provides a 12-week, small group study plan for looking at the practical aspects of personal financial management from a biblical perspective.

Donahue, Bill. *The Willow Creek Guide to Leading Life-Changing Small Groups.* Grand Rapids, Mich.: Zondervan, 1996. Bill Donahue considers a variety of aspects of small group operation including how to develop leaders, how to run a meeting, and how to provide care for those in the group.

Egan, Gerard. *Encounter: Group Processes for Interpersonal Growth.* Belmont, Calif.: Brooks/Cole Publishing Company, 1970. This book, written for professionals exploring the then-emerging use of encounter groups, provides an overview of the academic literature at that time.

Ellul, Jacques. *Money and Power.* Downers Grove, Ill.: InterVarsity Press, 1984. Jacques Ellul takes a provocative look at the relationship between money and power, particularly from a theological point of view.

Icenogle, Gareth Weldon. *Biblical Foundations for Small Group Ministry: An Integrational Approach.* Downers Grove, Ill.: InterVarsity Press, 1994. Gareth Icenogle, who pastors in Pennsylvania and also teaches at Fuller Theological Seminary, provides a unique discussion of small groups in a theological context.

Latourette, Kenneth Scott. *A History of Christianity.* New York, Harper and Brothers, 1953. This sweeping overview of church history from the founding through the early twentieth century includes descriptions of various movements in the church.

Mayer, David, Nancy Vogel, and George S. Johnson. *Starting Small Groups—and Keeping Them Going.* Minneapolis: Augsburg Fortress, 1995. This cooperative effort of leaders in the Evangelical Lutheran Church in America considers three aspects of small group activity: (1) understanding small groups; (2) organizing small groups in a church; and (3) training small group facilitators.

McBride, Neal F. Neal McBride, president of Grace University in Omaha, Nebraska, and author of *How to Have Great Small-Group Meetings* (Colorado Springs, Colo.: NavPress, 1997), has worked with small groups for some 25 years. His book explores the core idea that "great small group meetings happen by design, not default."

Mellis, Charles J. *Committed Communities: Fresh Streams for World Missions.* South Pasadena, Calif.: William Carey Library, 1976. In this volume Charles Mellis looks at the role that small groups have played in furthering the mission outreach of the church throughout its history.

Ministry of Money. Don McClanen serves as the director of the Ministry of Money, based in Gaithersburg, Maryland. The center publishes a regular newsletter that explores issues related to the handling of faith and money, offers workshops and retreats, and organizes "pilgrimages of reverse mission" to international sites.

Moore, Gary. Gary Moore, based in Sarasota, Florida, is an investment broker who has a particular concern for responsible investing from a Christian viewpoint. His first book was *The Thoughtful Christian's Guide to Investments* (Grand Rapids, Mich.: Zondervan, 1990).

O'Connor, Elizabeth. *Journey Inward, Journey Outward.* New York: Harper & Row, 1968. Elizabeth O'Connor describes the experience of the Church of the Saviour in Washington, D.C., as that group sought to combine the interior life with outreach. The first three chapters provide an overview discussion which may be of interest for someone who wants to do further reading on small groups.

Reid, Clyde. *Groups Alive—Church Alive: The Effective Use of Small Groups in the Local Church.* New York: Harper & Row, 1969. Clyde Reid was a staff member at the Institute for Advanced Pastoral Studies in Bloomfield Hills, Michigan. He also worked with small groups at Union Theological Seminary in New York. In this book, he shares his extensive experience with small groups. His book provides checklists and forms that can be copied, as well as a helpful analysis of dynamics.

Ronsvalle, John L., and Sylvia Ronsvalle. *Behind the Stained Glass Windows: Money Dynamics in the Church.* Grand Rapids, Mich.: Baker Books, 1996. The authors describe patterns evident as church leaders work to integrate faith and money. The book considers such issues as control dynamics, paradigmatic shifts affecting the context within which the church functions, and church member attitudes toward giving.

Rosenberg, Claude, Jr. Claude Rosenberg has written a book, *Wealthy and Wise: How You and America Can Get the Most out of Your Giving* (New York: Little, Brown and Company, 1994), that, while of value to the general reader, may be of particular interest to those with a combination of annual income greater than $265,000 and earning assets of more than $1.3 million.

Santa Ana, Julio de. *Good News to the Poor: The Challenge of the Poor in the History of the Church.* Maryknoll, N.Y.: Orbis Press, 1977. Julio de Santa Ana's main interest is how the church has responded to the poor throughout history. In the book's sixth chapter, this focus leads him to consider how the monastic movement addressed the theme of concern for the poor.

Sheely, Steve. *Director's Workbook for Small Groups.* Littleton, Colo.: Serendipity, 1994. The executive editor for this book is Lyman Coleman, a name often associated with small groups. This volume is part of the Serendipity library of materials. This particular volume provides information and practice exercises for those with responsibility for organizing and overseeing small groups. Serendipity also provides a wide-ranging series of resources for targeted groups such as singles, men's groups, youth and recovery groups.

_____. *Leader's Handbook for Small Groups*. Littleton, Colo.: Serendipity, 1994. In contrast to the director's group which helps design a small group structure, this book serves as an introduction for individuals who find themselves in the role of leading a small group.

Snyder, Howard A. *The Problem of Wineskins: Church Structure in a Technological Age*. Downers Grove, Ill.: InterVarsity Press, 1975. Howard Snyder considers the challenges of being the church in the current world environment, including the role that small groups play.

_____. *The Community of the King*. Downers Grove, Ill.: InterVarsity Press, 1977. Howard Snyder, currently at Asbury Theological Seminary, considers how the biblical concept of the kingdom of God interfaces with the modern church, including a brief discussion on small groups.

Turner, Nathan W. *Leading Small Groups: Basic Skills for Church and Community Organizations*. Valley Forge, Pa.: Judson Press, 1996. Nathan Turner has experience as both a pastor and clinical psychologist which he brings to bear on such topics as leadership skills and styles, stages of group development, and systems. He includes an entire chapter on conflict.

Williams, Dan. *Seven Myths About Small Groups: How to Keep from Falling into Common Traps*. Downers Grove, Ill.: InterVarsity Press, 1991. Besides exploring the seven misconceptions referred to in the title, Dan Williams also provides a variety of strategies for building a successful small group.

Wuthnow, Robert, ed. *"I Come Away Stronger": How Small Groups Are Shaping American Religion*. Grand Rapids, Mich.: William B. Eerdmans Publishing Company, 1994. A companion volume to *Sharing the Journey*, this book provides case studies of small groups which are functioning specifically within the religious context.

_____. *Sharing the Journey: Support Groups and America's New Quest for Community*. New York: The Free Press, 1994. This report covers the extensive research on small group activity in the United States done in the early 1990s by Robert Wuthnow of Princeton University's Center for the Study of American Religion.